HEARTS
CONNECT

Published by SoulSpring Publishing

Editor Jessica Hassan
Typesetting Islam Farid
Book Cover Harmony Art

ISBN 978-1-7394605-0-1
ISBN (ebook) 978-1-7394605-1-8

First edition 2023

hearts-connect.com

"This offering from Sister Sekina is one of the most important books of its time and will continue to be valuable for both Muslims and non-Muslims alike. Not only does this book map spiritual journeys and teaches principles relating to spirituality and building Islamic morals, but inside the pages of this book are stories of migration, race relation, history, belonging and intimate connection. This book is a reference point for so many intersections within society.

Through the tender facilitation of storytelling, Sekina has got to the root of what it means to be human and in pursuit of enlightenment. Whilst echoing the voice of many Black Muslims in the UK and some of the pathways to conversion, this book can easily sit on the shelves of academic institutions while at the same time be shared within family gatherings."

Muneera Pilgrim
Poet, author of *'That day she'll proclaim her chronicles'*,
writer, cultural producer and researcher

"This is a much-needed compilation that represents the diversity found within Muslim communities and the unique journey that leads to faith and spirituality. Sekina Yakub brings to life the importance of understanding intersectionality within those who share the Islamic faith. This is more than a collection of unique spiritual journeys, but a reflection of how the path to the search for truth can take many different forms, therefore encouraging the reader to embark on their own, unique spiritual awakening."

Yasmin Egala
Children's book author and creator of *'Treasures of Jannah'*
Co-founder of Tiny Mu'mins

"Sister Sekina Yakub has made a valuable and necessary addition to the archiving of stories of mostly, yet not exclusively British converts to Islam with her book Hearts Connect. The book focuses on the stories of young people of mostly African and Afro Caribbean descent, who by various paths found their way to Islam. The range of experiences in the stories are diverse - some people re-discovering an ancestral connection to Islam, others drawn by a search for God, a search for truth, clarity and simplicity.

The participants have shared honestly and movingly and the stories feel intimate and an honour to read. Sekina has handled each story with respect and dignity in her compilation and curation, each contributor's voice stands out clearly and distinctly. Sekina has woven a subtle and profound balance of personal narrative with scriptural and spiritual threads with her introductions, carefully selected ayats from the Quran, hadeeth, prayers & affirmations included with each story. After reading Hearts Connect, I'm left with a strong sense of the individual stories and history of Black Muslims in Britain (and a few stories from beyond Britain), the multiplicity of stories & experiences, all drawn to the central beacon of Tawheed and the Oneness of Allah."

Jumana Moon
Psychotherapist & Storyteller

"Have you heard the one about the curious history student, the hip hop artiste or the mother whose baby died? Well once you read Sekina Yakub's superbly researched and wonderful book you will come to know these and many other equally heartfelt stories. Stories of individuals and the path and mindset that led each of them to making a truly momentous decision to take on or change their religion. Yet every story is different, indeed unique. Yet it is possible to recognise one or two common themes, if you actually listen. One of my favourites is 'the catholic schoolgirl and the priest', but you'll make up your own mind."

Amal Abdalhakim-Douglas
Author of *'Call of the Twice Removed'*
Founder of Open Trade Network"

HEARTS CONNECT

'Narratives of Love, Trust and Surrender'

SEKINA YAKUB

SOULSPRING
PUBLISHING

May our hearts always connect!
Sekina Yakub

To Khadijah, Ahmad, Ibrahim and Sheikh.
Be the protagonist of your own stories.

Contents

Foreword

Recent research has revealed that Islam is the fastest growing religion in the United Kingdom. However, beneath the statistical data and media coverage lie the largely unheard voices of flesh and blood individuals and their personal narratives of religious conversion. In her book, Sekina Yakub adopts an approach that refrains from delving into the usual realm of psychology of religion or providing a purely intellectual analysis of the phenomenon of religious conversion. Rather, Yakub acknowledges that religious conversion is an intensely personal journey, resulting in profound philosophical, intellectual and spiritual transformations, as well as significant changes in an individual's social connections, lifestyle, values and ideological affiliations. By giving Muslim converts the pen to write their own stories, in their own words, Yakub presents a book that is rich in complexity, accurately capturing the diverse personal transformations and experiences of these individuals. The book answers important questions on the factors and processes that are powerful enough to lead and contribute to conversion to Islam in Britain.

Within the pages of this extraordinary book, Yakub takes us on an extraordinary voyage through the uncharted terrain of conversion to Islam in Britain. Here, amidst the anecdotes, reflections and revelations, lies an invaluable collection of silenced voices, courageous souls who have traversed the threshold of faith and emerged transformed.

Yakub, our intrepid guide on this captivating journey, adopts a unique and enlightened approach. She understands that religious conversion is far from a mere intellectual exercise or a detached analysis of statistical trends. No, it is a deeply personal odyssey that engenders profound philosophical shifts, spiritual awakenings and the reweaving of the very fabric of one's existence. It reshapes social connections, alters lifestyles and forges new pathways of purpose and meaning.

Through the gentle stroke of her pen, Yakub breathes life into the narratives of Muslim converts, granting them the power to recount their stories in their own words. In doing so, she illuminates the intricacies and complexities of their transformations, capturing the kaleidoscope of emotions, challenges and triumphs that accompany the journey of faith. From the depths of doubt and uncertainty to the luminous shores of conviction and belonging, each tale is a testament to the human capacity for resilience, growth and spiritual quest.

Within these pages, we find the answers to fundamental questions that pervade our collective consciousness. What are the catalysts that propel individuals towards Islam? What processes ignite the flame of conversion in the heart of Britain? As we delve deeper into this rich tapestry, we unravel the myriad factors that shape and mould these extraordinary journeys.

This book is not merely a compendium of stories; it is an invitation – a beckoning call to engage with narratives that defy conventional understanding. It challenges our preconceived notions, unveiling the profound humanity that resides within the diverse fabric of religious experiences. It is a testament to the power of faith and the transformative potential it holds for each and every one of us.

Sheikh M. Mumisa
Cambridge Special Livingstone Scholar
Trinity Hall, University of Cambridge

Preface

'There is no compulsion in religion. Indeed, the right path stands out clearly from error. Whoever rejects evil and believes in Allah has grasped the most trustworthy handhold that never breaks. Allah hears and knows all things.' Surah al-Baqarah, verse 256

WE know from the stories of the sahaba that the majority of those who found the message of the Prophet ﷺ appealing were young, mostly in their youth, in the prime of life. Children, in their innocence, easily see the truth, subhanallah. What links the stories in this anthology is that the contributors were mostly between the ages of sixteen and nineteen when they first felt a personal connection to Allah ﷻ. Though most grew up in religious households, the first experiential moment they felt their heart monumentally turn to Allah ﷻ was in their late adolescence, when temptations to engage in vices detrimental to their well-being were rife, and peer pressure was intense.

The following stories of self-discovery, belief and trust are not only an inspiration for future generations but also a testimony to these individuals' nurturing communities, who raised them to be such soul searchers. We cannot turn a blind eye to the fact that it takes a village to raise a child; the young adults who are present-day parents and grandparents show us the possibilities when we let the truth set us free. If we choose to adopt the right consciousness, it can only lead to success and excellence. Ameen.

"If the Day of Resurrection were established upon any one of you while he had in his hand a sapling, let him plant it."

Hadith of the Prophet Muhammad, narrated by Ahmad

Acknowledgements

I thank Allah the Most High for planting the seed of thought in my subconscious to embark upon putting together a string of personal narratives of incredible men and women whose strength to follow their heart and not the status quo is inspiring to so many. I would like to thank the following individuals for their time, patience and trust: Abdul Ahad, Abdullah Wilson, Adwoa Amina Ofori, Ahmad Ikhlas, Aishah B, Alison, Anthea Anisa Kissoon, Aziza White, Faizah Salihu, Imam Adeyinka Mendes, Iman Abdullah (Linda Roome), Inayah Amatullah, Ishmael Lea South, Leona Marius, Mario Da Barca (Mohammed Yayha), Mustafa Briggs, Patricia Harris-Seaton, Patricia Ruqayyah Harry, Rakin Fetuga Niass, Rashidah, Sukina Douglas, Sulaiman Aswad, Tzipporah Zainab Katunga, Umar Toure Julien and Umm Muhammad. I would also like to thank my editors Saaleh Patel and Jessica Hassan for their honest feedback (smiles) and encouraging words, my rock Rukayat for always going to lengths to support me and also Sheikh M. Mumisa and Hajj Amal AbdalHakim-Douglas for their invaluable advice.

Author's note

Connection is why we are here; it gives purpose to our lives. Neurobiologically, it is how we are wired, and when our hearts connect to the Most High, the All Knowing, the All Wise, we are at peace. Allah says, 'I did not create jinn or humankind except to worship me.' (51 adh-Dhariyat:16)

We cannot worship Him unless we have a connection to Him via the heart. Allah says, 'Neither my heavens nor my earth contain me, but the heart of my believing servant does contain me.' - Hadith Qudsi (A unique saying of Prophet Muhammad pbuh, its content is attributed to God but the actual wording is credited to the Prophet pbuh.)

Stories have been used over time to connect with others and to heal. The Qur'an is filled with stories that allow readers to make connections with the essence of the characters and thus use those ideals in their own lives. Each story in this collection is prefaced by a Qur'anic reference and concluded with a prophetic tradition linked to the story. Some names have been changed.

How we got to where we are

To understand the need for *Hearts Connect*, we need to peel back the layers of this £1 million question: 'Are you a convert or a revert?' Every born Muslim from Morocco to Indonesia has an ancestor who converted/reverted to the deen; every companion of the Prophet Muhammad (pbuh) chose to embrace the deen and so was a convert/revert. Originating as a term of endearment, convert/revert has over time become synonymous with a white or Black Muslim. For the ummah, this can be problematic and divisive as it very often conjures up a vulnerable Muslim with little knowledge of Allah, regardless of how long they have been in the deen of Islam. This, as evidenced by the companion, Abu Hurayra (ra), couldn't be further from the truth.

Abu Hurayra (ra) was the famous collector of the most ahadith – or sayings and actions of the Prophet Muhammad (pbuh). It is remarkable that Abu Hurayra (ra) 'converted' to the deen only three years prior to the Prophet (pbuh) passing from this world. Yet without his contribution to the deen of Islam, much of what we know about the Prophet (pbuh) would be unavailable, subhanallah. Would Abu Hurayra (ra) have been considered any less Muslim than others who converted within the first few years of the Prophet's twenty-three-year mission?

Born in the UK, I started practising the deen of Islam a few months short of my eighteenth birthday, and I immediately found myself surrounded by many Black British Muslims in

London. It is worth noting that the population of Muslims in the UK at the time was 3 percent, and the majority were South Asian migrants. Single ethnic groups would settle in a certain city or neighbourhood, for instance, the Yemeni Muslims in South Shields or the Bangladeshi Muslims in Tower Hamlets.

Civil wars and political persecution in Africa, the Middle East, South Asia and Eastern Europe since the 1980s led to the arrival of asylum seekers and refugees to the UK. This included Muslims from countries such as Algeria, Libya, Somalia, Iran, Iraq, Afghanistan and Bosnia.

In reality, Muslims were in Britain since the sixteenth century, when North African and Turkish galley slaves were released from ship from the Spanish Armada. English sailors, travellers and merchants also converted in Ottoman lands. However, from the late 1900s, the rapid growth of Muslims in Britain was by way of dockland communities in the port cities of London, Cardiff, Glasgow, Liverpool, Tyneside and Hull. This growth stemmed from colonial expansion activities. Britain's East India Company needed sailors for its trading ships, and while most seamen were Indian, cruel treatment and poor conditions in their home countries led Turks, Arabs, Somalis and Malays to join.

A significant number of these Muslims maintained their observance of Islamic practices while in Britain, such as the five daily prayers, fasting the month of Ramadan, organising travel for the pilgrimage, celebrating Eid and investing in mosques and burial arrangements. Another wave of Muslims in the post-war era of the 1960s and 1970s then entered Britain. Asian migrants who had settled in East Africa in the twentieth century no longer felt welcome in the newly independent countries of Kenya, Malawi, Tanzania and Uganda. Africa for the Africans policies were introduced in these countries, whereby many Indians found their opportunities restricted or faced deportation. The majority had British citizenship (obtained from India) and chose to make the UK their new home.

The 2001 census shows the ethnicities of Muslims in the UK as 67% Asian, 10% Black, 3% White, 5% European, 7% Arab, 4% other ethnic group and 4% mixed heritage. Migration, settlement, family life and the birth of children account for the vast majority of the growth of the UK's Muslim population. A minority, however, are converts/reverts (under 4%), who were not born nor socialised within Muslim families but made the conscious decision to adopt Islam as their religious identity, belief system and way of life. (There are others like myself who, though born into Muslim households, were ignorant of the religion and discovered it in their later years.)

In the late nineteenth century, a number of British travellers and intellectuals were first exposed to Islam through Muslim societies and made the decision to convert. They include but are not limited to Henry Quilliam, who travelled to and converted in Morocco (he returned to found the first mosque in Liverpool); Marmaduke Pickthall, a scholar of Islam who translated the Holy Qur'an into English and Lady Evelyn Cobbold, or Zainab as she was known. She was a Scottish noblewoman who had spent much of her childhood in North Africa and was the first British-born woman to undertake the hajj (pilgrimage) to Makkah. In this book you will find the stories of men and women, the majority of whom are from the African and Afro-Caribbean communities, who each made an individual spiritual choice to convert during the 1990s/2000s.

I feel it appropriate at this point to explain what a Muslim is, as an explanation for unfamiliar readers and a reminder for others. Each story exists within this framework. In Arabic, the word Muslim means one who willingly surrenders to God, and Islam means peace. Therefore, a Muslim is an individual who surrenders in peace to a religion of peace. You cannot force someone to submit; it has to be a personal choice, so this reduces the number of people who convert for other reasons. In order to become a practising Muslim, a person accepts the five pillars of Islam, which are the following:

1. Shahadah, to bear witness that 'There is no God but Allah and Muhammad (pbuh) is the last messenger of God,' which is a sincere declaration and profession of faith that will govern all actions in their life.

2. The five daily prayers, which are a compulsory form of worship that spiritually connects a Muslim to God, giving opportunities throughout the day to pause and seek forgiveness, comfort and guidance.

3. Paying zakat, which equals 2.5 percent of one's disposable wealth each year to help other Muslims who are in need. It is considered a spiritual duty.

4. Fasting the month of Ramadan, from dawn to dusk during the ninth month of the Islamic lunar calendar, which has many spiritual and health benefits.

5. Performing the hajj, which is a religious pilgrimage to Makkah in Saudi Arabia and is mandatory for all financially and physically capable adult Muslims at least once in their lives.

In addition to the five pillars of Islam, Islam also has six pillars of iman (faith), which also need to be accepted in order to complete one's identity as both a practicing and believing Muslim. The six pillars of faith are the following:

1. Belief in Allah (the Arabic name for the One God, as mentioned in the Qur'an). Everything is done with the intention of prioritising and pleasing God and complying with His laws.

2. Belief in angels, who were created before humans for the sole purpose of worshipping God. Angels are created from light and are not given the free will to do as they please.

3. Belief in the Books of God, which contain the message of the Oneness of God and serve as a moral and social guide to humankind. They include the Qur'an, Torah, Gospels and Psalms.

4. Belief in the prophets of God and that Muhammad (pbuh) is the last of them. Most of them were sent to specific nations with suitable teachings for those populations.

5. Belief in the Day of Judgement, when everyone will be resurrected and questioned about their deeds, actions and beliefs. The day of complete justice and recompense.

6. Belief in God's divine decree and that everything happens according to His Will. Our actions and desires (dua) for a specific outcome, however, can change our divine decree.

Ihsan (striving for excellence) is the third main basis of the religion, which essentially involves doing one's best in all affairs, being aware that Allah is seeing you.

With the many references to the Nation of Islam in this book, I'd like to add a statement by Minister Louis Farrakhan: 'We are practicing Islam as we know and understand it. The pillars of faith are the same as are the pillars of Practice: we practice prayer, fasting, charity and hajj as the Prophet taught them. The difference that makes us seem unorthodox is that The honourable Elijah Muhammad addressed a psychological condition of 400 years of misteachings that caused us to hate the colour of our skin, the kinkiness of our hair, the thickness of our lips, the broadness of our noses and our African origin in this world. He had to reverse that, so he taught us the glory of being Black and this to many orthodox Muslims was against the teachings of Islam because Islam does not deal with colour. However, the Quran is called a healing so here we are a people sick with self hatred so surely in the book the Quran there is a healing for the sickness or ill of self hatred. These are considered unorthodox methods but we are as Muslim as any Muslim that is Muslim.'

For readers who may not be familiar with the Black struggle and the idea of people of African descent arming themselves with self-love, here is a brief history to set the context from which many of these stories emerge. It is also important to be aware that some of our best efforts for gender equality and striving for this deen historically come from Africa.

Over 400 years ago, millions of Africans were abducted from their homes in Africa, taken across the Atlantic and made to work as slaves in the Americas. In order to accomplish this mission effectively, the enslaved underwent 'seasoning' to break their will; they were subjected to horrific persecution and refused access to education, an identity (their birth name), their language and religion – all the facets that made them who they were. Years of continuous subjugation and deep emotional and physical trauma resulted in what is termed post-traumatic stress disorder (PTSD). This has affected generations of Blacks in the US, the Caribbean and Britain, many of whom were without formal support (counselling/therapy). They faced and overcame this collective pain, and they experienced post-traumatic growth. When pain won't let you give up on yourself, it gives you strength. Knowing the pain experienced by their ancestors – seeing loved ones murdered before their very eyes and being separated from family members and knowing they had no rights since they were owned – affected their autonomy. Due to all of this, in addition to the understanding that, till today, many blacks are not seen as equals in Western countries, many deem the ummah a refuge.

After the official abolition of slavery in 1778, it took a further one hundred years before slavery ended in practical terms. However, Black people were not provided with the same rights as their fellow white counterparts; instead, they were to accept a humiliating social and economic system of sharecropping, a lack of education and Jim Crow laws of segregation. They were treated as subhuman hundreds of years after the abolition of slavery, despite the US constitution statement 'all men are created equal'. And it didn't end there. From the 1980s, the Black race faced systematic mass incarceration in the US (lawful slavery), which included the school to prison pipeline, the three strikes law and the war on drugs.

The civil rights movement saw an end to laws separating Blacks and Whites, but it would take more than laws to provide Black people with a level playing field emotionally and economically. Eventually, between the 60s and 90s, a mass movement grew to encourage Black pride and self-love after years of people being deemed worthless and sometimes not visible at all. With this arose figures like Angela Davis and Stokely Carmichael (Kwame Tura), and in 1965, Ruby Bridges was the first child legally permitted to attend a white school. She had to be escorted to class by police because of people's hatred and their fear of what it would mean for White America. Growing up aware of all this, knowing you lack representation in the media and always feeling like an 'other' was difficult; this made people that much more excited during the 80s and 90s when it became 'cool' to be Black. Blacks were becoming financially well off, and various markets, like the beauty, fashion and entertainment industries, were competing to become beneficiaries of their disposable income. All of this is the backdrop to many of the stories you will read.

These are the stories of Muslims whose paths I have crossed. I share some of their journey, which may not be as grandiose and far-reaching as that of Abu Hurayra (ra), but they certainly are extremely inspiring. I have let each voice choose the term they prefer to identify with: convert, revert or just Muslim. Most have opted for the abbreviation pbuh for 'peace and blessings be upon him' after mentioning the Holy Prophet's name; others have used the Arabic phrase ﷺ. I pray that each story is a source of comfort to us, our children and future generations. I hope it goes some way in showing an appreciation for one another's struggles and triumphs in the search for the comfort of the soul. When you know where you've been, you feel empowered knowing what you've been through, and it pushes you to accomplish more in life without as much fear.

They say it's not always easy, but it always is worth it. May this book serve as a window to illustrate the power of love we have, the belief we have in ourselves for the truth and how we hold each other dear, important and seen in our hearts. I also hope it demonstrates the sincere sacrifice and real commitment individuals undertake for their love of God. The Prophet Muhammad (pbuh) said to his companions 'I wish I could meet my brothers.' The companions asked, 'Are we not your brothers?' He replied, 'No, you are my companions; my brothers are those who will come into the world after me and have faith in me although they never saw me.' Hearts connect for the sake of God. We gratefully recognise where we have come from, know where we are and anticipate where we are heading in sha Allah (God willing).

I

Sowing seeds of change

'We will show them Our signs in the horizons and within themselves until it becomes clear to them that it is the Truth.' (41 Fussilat:53)

M any from the Caribbean community have been drawn to Islam for a variety of reasons, but it is a common occurrence that having transcended all there is to be 'had' from following society's whims, a gaping hole is realised that couldn't be filled. This is Abdullah's story.

I was interested in the Nation of Islam,[01] in particular the great orator Malcolm X and the doctrine he espoused and also the US rapper Ice Cube (O'Shea Jackson). The film *Malcolm X* had just been released, and it was 1993. The hype around the film drew me into the X paraphernalia, and I bought a Malcolm X cap to show my solidarity with his cause. It was black with a large white X on the front. I felt uplifted and woke to Black consciousness when I had it on. I wore it proudly around my college campus, and one day a Moroccan guy approached me. He started up a conversation with me about Malcolm X; at first his talk was light and casual, and we were in agreement. I was surprised by his awareness, but then he delved a bit deeper, past

---

[01] A religious and political organisation founded in the US in 1930 by Wallace Fard Muhammad.

Malcolm's rhetoric on Black nationalism and touched on Islam, the foundation of knowing yourself on a spiritual level. He asked if I knew that Malcolm X was a Muslim and that he followed the faith called Islam after his break from the Nation of Islam? My response was nonchalant, so he then started to explain what Islam is. He proceeded to illustrate the fact that the Nation of Islam was quite different to Islam. Now I was intrigued.

He was a few years older than I was, and we didn't share any of the same classes, but we often bumped into each other around the college. Every time we met, we carried on our conversation, which became less about Malcolm and more about the faith he followed. I soon realised the subject was inexhaustive.

One day he invited me over to his house, as he clearly had more to share. I was open to knowing more about Islam, so I readily accepted the invitation. This led to more invites and more opportunities to not only hear about Islam but *see* it practically too. Through these interactions, I was fortunate enough to catch glimpses of Islam operating in his home and in the manner in which he and his family ate, prayed and communicated with each other. He lived with his wife and two children, and I found myself looking forward to seeing them as it all seemed like a good harmonious setup to me; both husband and wife appeared to be on the same page because they shared a spiritual affinity. I was nineteen years old at the time, living at home with my parents, who were quite laid back religiously. My mother attended church services every week; my father didn't. So seeing the commitment of this guy and his wife, I couldn't help but appreciate how Islam made their lives easier; they were in spiritual agreement.

Looking back, I was definitely searching for a path of guidance even though I wasn't fully aware that I was. I had felt a strong dissatisfaction with my life up to that point because I believed I had explored most things. For instance, clubbing and personal relationships. I wasn't one to choose to drink alcohol or take drugs, so I couldn't figure out what else there was to experience in life. I just knew in my heart this couldn't be all there was, so I intentionally sought out the Moroccan guy; I found him interesting to talk to. I couldn't ignore the interest in Islam pulling at my heart.

As if by some twist of fate, I suddenly discovered that someone who lived close to me had embraced Islam. He was a white fella who liked rap music and was considered cool. I felt an impulse to reach out to ask him questions and find out more. When I did, it turned out there were others who had also entered the faith, and they all gladly spoke to me about it whenever I met them. It was a pleasant experience; all of a sudden, I was attracting Muslims to me from all directions. There were some ethnic Muslims who had recently started practising and a couple of New Muslims who were sharing an apartment, so I often visited their place to talk to them. They were approachable and really relatable. One of them sensed I was hungry and ready for more and gave me a copy of an English translation of the meaning of the Holy Qur'an, which I took home and began to read.

I became fascinated with it because I hadn't been much of a Bible reader. My main concepts of God and religion had come from my Caribbean roots. I found reading the Qur'an very different to anything I had ever experienced. It was very clear; it gave me clarity, particularly in the main area of tawheed – the Oneness of God. For instance, Surah Ikhlas is exceptionally straightforward in its message.

I benefited a lot from the Moroccan guy giving me explanations of verses from the Qur'an. I didn't know if they came from his own understanding or from a scholar's perspective, but it gave me a foundation to the fundamental basics of Islam.

From then on, my journey to Islam was through learning about and understanding the Qur'an. I chose not to have too many friends around me; it was a deliberate solo journey. My schedule was made up of working during the day, learning from the Moroccan guy some evenings and visiting the Muslims' apartment on the weekends, while my non-Muslim friends were out clubbing.

Being exposed to Islam at the Moroccan man's home was probably what appealed to me the most. Because I like hygiene, I appreciated the instinja[02] concept. Going into their bathroom, I thought, 'Wow, Islam even goes into how to use the toilet!' I thought this was really a good way of life. I liked the family lifestyle and the way he interacted with his wife and children. I observed the fact that his wife was there getting on with family matters, which meant less hassle for the relationship than her just going out doing her own thing without consideration for her loved ones. That can put a relationship in turmoil. From my past, I observed that a lot of arguments can arise when you are out clubbing with your partner. Someone usually got drunk, and the night ended in a quarrel of some sort. All of this was removed from the equation.

In hindsight, I didn't realise that there are disagreements within the home regardless of your religious affiliation. I had rose-tinted glasses on back then because it was all so new to me. I was looking through a 'grass is greener' lens, and I was not really focused on the husband-wife personal dynamics that come into play when part of a union. At that moment, I was fixated on the Qur'an, understanding it and seeing it portrayed before me. I was focused on the Faultless; inevitably humans all have faults. We are perfectly imperfect.

I later discovered that there were many different ethnicities living side by side in my area; there were Yemenis, Pakistanis, Bengalis and Somalis, to name a few, all worshipping the same God. Although I knew they were all Muslim, I used to consider them more as ethnic groups than followers of a religious persuasion. I was gaining clarity. Looking back, I realised I must have also had many Muslim friends at primary school, but religious nuances weren't something we noticed in our friendship groups back then.

Whenever I visited the young men's apartment, I enjoyed the atmosphere; it was lighthearted and jovial, but I knew I wasn't

---

[02] Islamic term for the obligatory action of using water to clean oneself after urinating and/or defecating. Toilet paper can be used in addition.

really looking for a social group as I already had friends and I also came from a large family. I was not coming into Islam for friends; I was looking for the Truth. Watching the film *Malcolm X* had sparked this interest; it made me curious about the Nation of Islam and their unflinching discipline. I admired their Black self-love and their re-education of concepts that had long been accepted as fact and never questioned throughout the generations.

I still value the power of language and the awareness of racial bias in everyday words as highlighted by Malcolm X. He introduced me to the dictionary definitions of 'black' and 'white', which presuppose black as inherently evil and wrong and white as good and pure. I found this remarkable, as it is assumed that the dictionary is objective. I realised it is actually racist and supports white supremacy. But it is not real; it's just the way the establishment has depicted the definitions of words, which enter our subconscious for better or worse. This then influences how people feel and understand words. For example, a white lie is harmless, whereas a black market is illegal.

Ice Cube was also someone who heavily influenced my journey as I listened to many of his early tracks, which he wrote when part of the Nation of Islam. A lot of the philosophy came through in his lyrics; he was and still is an extremely talented artist, and it was alluring when he spoke about the establishment being racist and not for us, the masses. He answered many of the questions I had swimming around my head. He helped me understand why things were the way they were, why Black self-worth was low and what could be done about it. There had only been a small scene in *Malcolm X* that depicted his transition from Nation of Islam to Islam, which climaxed with his pilgrimage to Mecca. So I was only aware of his incarceration, spirituality and self-discovery through the lens of the film. I only really knew the Nation of Islam side of him until I met the Moroccan guy.

I also found Islam appealing because I wasn't told to 'turn the other cheek', as propagated by Martin Luther King Jr. I respected him, but his stance against social injustice was clothed in Christian rhetoric, which I saw as disempowering for the people. In Islam, if you see an evil act, you try to change it and if you cannot, you hate it in your heart and that is the weakest of faith. The Christian idea that I should turn the other cheek in the face of oppression didn't sit comfortably with me at all. My heart wrestled with that. I felt I would rather stand strong and say wrong is wrong and fight back.

Just before I took my shahadah, I did have some reservations on a couple of areas of Islam, but they weren't paramount because I still embraced Islam. I found my heart really drawn to accept first and then have those issues clarified for me afterwards. In other words, I had to step inside the safety of the house first to understand how some things operated.

After taking my shahadah, I started practising Islam. To take it on properly, I felt the need to break some old habits. I cut off relationships with women, and I distanced myself from my old friends for a long time. I couldn't juggle practising Islam and hanging out with them. I then forged new friendships with Muslims, and we had a good group of about fifteen of us. The more I learnt, it gradually dawned on me that being Caribbean, I already knew there was a God from my upbringing; however, Islam undeniably gave me the clarity and peace of mind I needed. I saw it was better to follow the commands of God now that I knew what was expected of me, and I didn't think I was depriving myself of anything because I was already disillusioned with my old life and the limits on what was available.

Shortly after taking my shahadah, I was invited to a church by one of my closest friends. I went along and I felt the sermon was very good, as if the preacher was talking directly to me, and my heart wrestled with that. Many Christians I knew based their experience with God on how it felt to them to have God speak to them directly. When they felt a connection, their belief was strong; when they didn't, they felt forsaken. I decided to discuss this with a pastor, but his response didn't really make sense to me, and when I brought up the same incident to the Muslims around me, their explanations were clearer and deeper, which also confirmed I was in the right place.

When I first began practising, I admit I did get quite Arabised and colonised by the Pakistanis with regards to my dress and appearance, as I thought it was the only way to be Muslim. Most of the brothers around me were into politics and were very intellectual, so turning back to jahiliyyah[03] was constantly refuted; it was not something I could even consider. A brother and I embraced Islam within a week of each other, so this aided our journey as we were in the same position, going through similar experiences that we often shared. I derived comfort in knowing I wasn't alone and could share what was going on with someone I knew would understand. That was a huge blessing.

As a Muslim, my interest in the Nation of Islam waned, despite their ruthless activism in fighting against violations of human rights, because I knew the racist aspect at its core didn't work for me. I had some good white mates. I knew I would be contradicting myself if I delved in further because I was cool and comfortable with my white friends. I knew its message wasn't right, but I did appreciate some of the other goals it stood for, such as providing Black people with the encouragement and strength to believe and stand up for themselves and to educate themselves and build their own communities to achieve self-sufficiency as a Black nation rather than just being tools of entertainment – there's more to us than that.

In my opinion, opportunities for traditional education on Islam in the West are still lacking for someone interested in the faith. Even though it is straightforward, you need to go through 'aqeeda[04] and some basic fiqh[05] to get you going. I struggled through some clumsy translations, and it could have been easier for me. When I embraced Islam, naturally there was mention

---

[03] The condition of ignorance and disbelief before coming to Islam.

[04] Islamic creed or theology.

[05] Jurisprudence, the body of Islamic law extracted from Islamic sources, namely the Qur'an and ahadith (saying and actions of the Prophet Muhammad ﷺ).

made about my name, but I felt I was not a dog who could be named by someone else, so I chose one myself from a book of Muslim names.

Prophetic Tradition

'The world is a prison for the believer and a paradise for the disbeliever.' (Sahih Muslim)

Supplication/Affirmation

I open my heart to the words of Allah.

2

Advice from a priest

'And when they hear what has been revealed to the Messenger, you see their eyes overflowing with tears because of what they have recognised of the Truth.'
(5 al-Maidah:83)

For many who come from a strong religious background and hear the message of Islam, it can turn their world upside down. Often a process of grief for the loss of what was known ensues, which leads to anger, then denial creeps into the heart until acceptance is found within. This is Leona's story.

I was born on Good Friday, 20 April, in London's St Thomas Hospital, a blessed day due to it being the Christian holy season of Easter. By the time I had fully transitioned from Catholicism to Islam, my birthday had already landed six times on one of these holy days where the focus is heavily on Jesus (as). I was baptised and raised as a Catholic in Southwest London.

I attended St Mary's Primary School in Clapham Common, which split the boys and girls up after Reception class. Then I attended Notre Dame, an all-girls secondary school in Battersea that was run by nuns. After one year, my all-girls school amalgamated with an all-boys school, but there was no escaping the nuns, because they came too.

My upbringing and schooling was very much Catholic, and despite not acting very Catholically, having to share some of my birthdays with Jesus (as) made the bond between us very special. This religious indoctrination from birth gave me all the beliefs, ideas, structure and methods to live a so-called good life without knowing any difference. I was aware of other religions, such as Hinduism, Buddhism and the Jehovah's Witnesses but only because they had noticeable traits. I would notice the bindi worn on the forehead of the Hindu; the robe, cymbals and humming of the Buddhists as they walked barefoot in the middle of the road; and the knocking on the front door of the Jehovah's Witnesses, who never could take the hint that they had overstayed their welcome. I had no knowledge of any of their beliefs.

In April or May of the year I was a fifth-year student, I was taking my final exams, and I had no more classes or school. I had just turned sixteen. I sat in the front room, bored at home, when I decided to pull out one of the volumes from my mother's collection of Bible stories. These were light blue on top and dark blue at the bottom, clearly numbered in white print. They looked crisp and new, just like the first day she bought them all those years ago. I read a Bible story about the condemnation of a man who had spent the previous night in the presence of a holy man. However, the very next day the holy man shunned him because he had eaten the flesh of swine. As well as this, I read the story of the holy man casting demons into the same animals. I couldn't believe that the same people who had been teaching me Catholicism were feeding me this cursed meat. This saw the beginning of the end of Catholicism for me. Abstinence from eating the cursed meat that I once loved was instant, extremely easy, and done purely with the faith of a sixteen-year-old Catholic me.

Next, I encountered an event in my life that took a mental, physical and emotional toll on me. This, rightfully so, caused my sanity to be questioned by many. I now know that this was another part of my transitional process from Catholicism to Islam.

The first person I turned to was Jesus (as). I declared my love and allegiance to him. I made all kinds of promises and commitments to him. I reminded him that my birthday was close to Easter. Instead of blowing out candles on a delicious birthday cake, I had to have fish cakes. Instead of everyone's attention being on me, they were deep in remembrance of him. However, I told him that I wanted to be just like him and be devoted in prayer just like him.

As I was about to pray *to* Jesus (as), it dawned on me that there was one huge problem. This definitely was a game changer. I realised that after all the church masses, the Religious Education literature read at school and the same 1977 Jesus of Nazareth movie for the past thirteen years, not once had I questioned the different scripts where Jesus (as) calls for help: 'My God, my God, why have you forsaken me?' Alarm bells rang through my head; red flags waved between my eyes. I gathered that if 'Lord' Jesus, 'Christ', 'the son of God', 'our saviour' required divine intervention, then this could only mean one thing. He had a boss!

For the first time ever, I realised that there was a divine hierarchy. There was an Almighty deity who was helping Jesus (as), and all I knew was that I needed His help too. I set out on my quest the following morning to find the Almighty deity. For some strange reason, just like Prophet Ibrahim (as), I had an inclination as to which characteristics the Almighty would and would not possess, but I just didn't know where or how to find Him. The obvious question that I needed to ask was 'Who was Jesus (as) praying to?'

The next morning, I hastily left home for the short walk to my church. Annoyingly, the gates were shut, but in their defence, it was only 5.40 a.m. I completed at least three more rounds of this journey before eventually gaining access to the church. I excitedly presented my question to the priest. 'Who was Jesus (as) praying to?'

Eventually, I spoke to two different priests in my church who both gave me responses that I found unsatisfactory and illogical.

I took the same question to the Seventh-day Adventists, the Jehovah's Witnesses and at least two other places of worship of different denominations. They either said Jesus (as) was God, he was the Lord, he was the son of God, he was the lamb of God or he was Christ who cleaned the world of all our sins by dying on the cross.

As a teenager who used logic, I knew that there was no way Jesus (as) died in vain. In my opinion, the world definitely had bad guys doing bad things; therefore, the world wasn't clean of sin. As well as this, I pondered on Jesus's (as) words while on the cross 'My God, my God, why have you abandoned me?' (Matthew 27:46 and Mark 15:34).

In my view, the Almighty deity did not make mistakes. To sacrifice Jesus (as) for our sins and to still have sin enshroud us would surely be a mistake. This would definitely be an error of judgement on the Almighty's behalf, and my Almighty deity had better judgement than that. Was Jesus (as) not someone so precious to Him? Could He not save Jesus (as)? Or was Jesus (as) being ignored? These questions were yet to be answered.

Following on with my line of enquiry, I posed new questions. If Jesus (as) was God or the Lord, why would there be a need to pray to another God for help? If Jesus (as) is God, why did he implant himself inside a woman's womb to be born as a human and then spend most of his time praying for someone else's intervention to get him out of situations? If Jesus (as) is the lamb of God, then what does that even mean?

Unfortunately, people lost patience with me. I could sense their frustration with the tangles we were getting into. They had not imagined how hard it would be to convince a vulnerable teenage girl that she should just accept their speech and join their service. Disappointed that my mission had failed, I did begin to pray to the 'whoever Jesus (as) was praying to' deity. That went on until one day, when a certain young man on the street spoke to me.

I later came to understand that he had intentionally stood idly on the side of the pavement waiting for me to approach his path. He had been sleeping in the mobile shop on security duty and had noticed my journeys back and forth to the church. Unbeknownst to me, he had even observed that initial 5.40 a.m. journey. Once I had shared with him how I was in search of who Jesus (as) was praying to, he ushered me inside the mobile shop where he had a quiet word with someone in the back room.

In no time, a large, heavy book (the Qur'an) was presented to me and part of its contents were read. Immediately, without a shadow of a doubt, I had found the name for my 'whoever you are that Jesus (as) was praying to' deity. The deity's name was Allah and He was the one Jesus (as) sought help from! All was good, until this joy of mine was shattered, just by the bare mention of Prophet Muhammad ﷺ.

My line of thought was: 'Who is this? What is this? Never ever had the sound waves of this blessed name been absorbed by my ears before.' Then I began thinking, 'Besides, I love Jesus (as), I only know Jesus (as), and I don't care about anyone else.' I could not deny nor hide that I was convinced that the Almighty deity Allah was the one. I was comforted by the fact that Jesus (as) is mentioned in the Qur'an many times as Esa (as). However, I could not accept that anyone came after Jesus (as).

That night, I pondered my discoveries. I reflected on how my parish priest was wrong, those people in the mobile shop were right, Allah was most definitely the Almighty deity and my love for Jesus (as) was definitely not going anywhere. I stumbled terribly at the prospect of Prophet Muhammad ﷺ being added to the mix. He did not have any significance in my conscious thoughts. I had no knowledge of him throughout my life so far, and I knew that I needed to go back to those who taught me my religion to resolve this dilemma.

By this time, I was already seventeen, so I made the journey back to the school that I had graduated from the year before. I intended to confront Mr Walsh, my religious education teacher. He was my last hope. Arriving outside of the staff room, I tapped on the door until a member of staff opened it. Mr Walsh was not there, so I had to opt for someone else. My ex-Geography teacher appeared on the other side of the door. I just blurted out 'Sir, I just wanted to know who Jesus (as) was praying to, I feel a bit confused.' He told me to go in haste to my old tutor's room, where I would find a priest who was just about to leave.

I was near to the room when I spotted the priest along the corridor heading towards the stairway to the exit. I picked up my pace and managed to swing my whole body in the precise position I needed to block the path of the priest. Oddly enough, he did not seem phased by my behaviour; on the contrary, it seemed more like he had been expecting me.

In the room, we sat opposite each other. With the surroundings familiar to me, I felt at ease. We made our introductions before I delivered my entire story. I recall getting to the point where I informed him that the people in the mobile shop tried to fool me into believing how some person came after Jesus (as). I reassured him that I wasn't buying that part of the story; therefore, he need not worry. However, what happened next could have knocked me off my seat. The priest, who was obviously an excellent listener because he had not once interrupted me, responded by saying, 'Yes, they have told you the truth, Prophet Muhammad ﷺ did come after Jesus (as).'

After the initial shock, I was left speechless. Checking to see if I had heard incorrectly, I asked him to repeat what he had just said. He did better than that, he gave me an exact number of years that Prophet Muhammad ﷺ arrived after Jesus (as). He told me Jesus's (as) purpose and that Jesus (as) did in fact mention the coming of Prophet Muhammad ﷺ. He told me why Prophet Muhammad ﷺ had come and that he had come for all nations, whereas Jesus (as), just like Moses (as) and the other prophets, had come for specific parts of the world.

Unconsciously, I began to speak my thoughts. The unwinding of a movie reel had physically started taking place within my brain. Everything my faith was once based on was being reversed and somehow undone. The 1977 'Jesus of Nazareth' film, which was often broadcast twice in one day. The partaking of three religious ceremonies, including my baptism in the name of Jesus (as); my first holy communion at seven or eight years old, where I consumed the symbolism of the body and blood of Christ (bread and fake wine) and my confirmation at fifteen years of age, where I affirmed my faith in Jesus (as).

Feelings of bewilderment turned into deceit. This had a chilling effect that numbed my brain; I just could not fathom the deception. Now, being conscious of my thoughts, I made sure this priest told me exactly what he knew. Unknowingly, like military personnel, I began to interrogate him. First question: 'Why is this not in the Bible?' The Priest, without hesitation informed me that the Bible is one version out of many that had been written after Jesus (as).

Every single question I asked was answered to my satisfaction and was logical. I could not fault him. For example, in his answers, he made reference to the similarities of the Orthodox Christians' and Muslims' attire, in that they both wear modest clothing with head coverings and long dresses. As a matter of fact, I had recently travelled to Cyprus and saw two nuns and later saw two Muslim ladies. It was difficult to distinguish who were the nuns and who were the Muslims. This was due to the nuns being dressed in what looked exactly like the hijab and abaya of the Muslims.

Astounded by these revelations, I believe I may have unconsciously asked my next question. With dazed eyes, I stared at his dog collar (also known as a clerical collar) and asked 'Why are you a priest?' In his perfectly fitting answer, he gave me some indication that he was not teaching any of those different versions of the Bible that were known to me, which made me believe that I may have missed the hint that he was letting me in on a secret.

Wrapping up my consultation with the priest, before we departed, he praised me for my research, acknowledging my determination and quest for the Truth. He was adamant that I should remain guided on the right path. He assured me that I will increase my trust and faith when I increase my knowledge. He then gave me one last crystal clear and concise instruction to be carried out with immediate effect: 'Go back to the mobile shop and take your shahadah.'

So bewildered by the events that took place, I asked what a shahadah was, and he told me to accept their path. I then asked where I could find him again. He replied that he was only a visitor preparing to go back to his country within days (could have been Austria or Cyprus. I cannot be sure, but he did not have an accent). He told me that he was staying in the church next door to the school. It took some time to process, but I really couldn't remember there ever being a church next door to the school.

Back in Clapham Common, I marched myself into my Catholic church to speak to the priest. I demanded to know why he hadn't told me all this information that I just accumulated from the mysterious priest (MP). As I relayed the conversation I had with MP, the Catholic priest kept probing for information leading to the identity and whereabouts of MP! To be honest, I had not taken much notice of MP's name, and right about now this priest in front of me was starting to freak me out. He was sounding more and more like a mobster and less and less like a holy man of God. He made a command to 'wait there'.

A sense of fear came over me as I was sure he went to call for backup. I was afraid. I wasn't waiting to be bundled into the back of a van nor strapped into a white straitjacket, so I took flight towards the exit doors. Glancing over my shoulder, I legged it out of the church grounds as fast as I could, and that saw the ending of Catholicism for me.

Taking refuge in the mobile shop, I was safe and sound, and there I took my shahadah. They gave me a Qur'an, which I read from cover to cover, and I learnt how to pray. My confidence grew because I read and pondered the Qur'an and developed a strong relationship with Allah. I was now knowing, trusting and believing more than ever before. Reading the Qur'an increased my understanding and helped me heal tremendously. I developed an understanding from it, including the realisation that when I read the same section over again, it would have a different connection to my knowledge and understanding. This is when I started to realise the power of the Qur'an and that it was indeed for a nation and not for just an individual.

I physically met my sheikh[06] in Ramadan when I was one month away from my eighteenth birthday. He is my spiritual mentor. He trained me to use my heart to communicate, and not my mouth, and this is how the heart connection between us developed. The process of this was not as simple as it sounds, because I was not aware of what was taking place.

I wanted to voice my views, opinions and comments freely to my sheikh with my gobby little teenage mouth, but no matter how hard I tried, no sound would come out. I knew he was doing this to me, and I felt deflated and really broken inside. Until one day, while he was walking up the stairs, he turned his head towards me and gave a knowing smile with knowing eyes. I immediately knew that this transaction was concerning a harmless lesson of adab, as well as it being better to use my heart instead of my mouth. But there was something else lurking behind the knowing eyes! It was at this point that I saw a resemblance or just had a realisation that Sheikh either knew about MP or he *was* MP!

This was when I realised that my journey to Islam had not begun the day I ran out of the church and straight into the mobile shop. It had begun the day I picked up the Bible story and stopped eating pork at sixteen years old, when I was technically still a Catholic. Upon reflection, being depicted as a crazy person was to my benefit. I had to go through this ordeal in order to become who I am today. It allowed me to see how people behaved towards me and others.

I saw fake and real people. As long as people believed me to be crazy, they were *not* watching their behaviour around me. Little did they know that I was observing every aspect about them. With all my personal teachings from Allah, I was armoured

---

[06] Also spelt shaykh, shaikh and cheikh, it is an honorific title in the Arabic language.

with unbreakable knowledge, understanding and a special connection. I heeded for no one. Does Allah not say that he gives knowledge to whomever He wills?

Overall, I am extremely pleased with my journey into Islam. I know that it's right. My message to all those Muslims imposing their culture on us is that it is not Islam. My advice to new Muslims is to take your time and concentrate on developing a relationship with Allah Almighty. My advice to Muslims who are not new is to be good role models to new Muslims and non-Muslims. Your job is not to command anyone to do anything that they are not ready to do nor should you be sanctimonious.

My biggest regret is following the command to change my name; there was no need. We existed in the soul realm where we all affirmed to Allah that we were going to do everything that is right on earth; changing your name is not going to help you. It's about being good people, being the best hearted people and following the way of Prophet Muhammad ﷺ and ultimately returning to Allah pure.

Prophetic Tradition

'Whoever calls others to guidance, then he will receive a reward similar to whoever followed him without it decreasing from either of them.' (Sahih Muslim)

Supplication/Affirmation

Oh Allah, Knower of the unseen and the seen, I am grateful for all that I am, all that I have and all that I have been through.

3

What's in a name?

'Call them by the names of their fathers; it is more just in the sight of Allah. But if you do not know their fathers – then they are still your brothers in religion.' (33 al-Ahzab:5)

When you read, see or hear a message more than once, you don't witness something in it that wasn't there before; you observe something in you that wasn't there before. This is Ahmad's story.

I grew up in a Christian household with my father, uncles, aunties and grandparents. We all lived together, and my grandmother was my primary carer. It was a large house, the centre of many big gatherings with relatives for birthdays, Christenings, Christmas and Easter, so there was a definite presence of Christianity, God and gratitude in our home, but we were not overly strict.

When I was younger, the bus would arrive to pick up my younger brother and I to take us to Bible study. At Sunday school, we were sectioned off into different age groups and learnt to read the Bible and reflect on it. There were many stories that stuck in my mind: the flood of Noah (as), the parting of the Red Sea by Moses (as), the virgin birth and miracles of Jesus (as) and the consequences of Cain and Abel. I always felt I could learn direct lessons from these stories, and later on, when I discovered Islam and its similar narratives, it didn't feel alien to me. It felt very familiar because of my childhood knowledge.

While growing up, I saw a lot of Muslims; however, I didn't identify with them or see any similarities between what they and I believed until I intentionally began to look closer at Islam. That was when I found out that there were many stories told to me during my time as a Christian that were almost identical to stories in the Qur'an. I thought 'Wow, this is interesting; this is the same, or rather an extension of what I used to believe!' In this way, I saw Islam as giving me more clarity of mind.

I noticed a few visible Muslims, and in addition to the Pakistani and Arab Muslims around me, I had one Caribbean Muslim friend. In discussions with him, he helped me see that I could be Muslim as well if I wanted; it wasn't an Asian religion, akin to Hinduism[07], Jainism[08] or Sikhism,[09] where the followers shared the same language and culture as the faith. I assumed all these religions were only adopted by people from the Indian subcontinent, so knowing this wasn't the case with followers of Islam made me curious, and I gave myself permission to imagine my life as a Muslim.

I was fifteen going on sixteen when I began to gain a proper awareness of Islam, and for a time, my older sister also showed an interest and introduced me to more of its concepts. She even went to the mosque and told me about it, and I thought it sounded really fascinating. In the 1990s, there was a whole Black awareness phenomenon building up, where we heard buzzwords like 'Malcolm X',[10] 'Allah', 'Muslim' and 'Muhammad'. With the success of the critically acclaimed movie *Malcolm X*, merchandise like T-shirts and caps became cool to wear. It also became a sign of awareness for a Black person of African descent

---

[07] An Indian religion and way of life that teaches reincarnation, the third largest religion with 1.2 billion followers.

[08] Teaches that the path to enlightenment is through nonviolence and that reincarnation is determined by one's karma.

[09] Originated in the Punjab region of India around the fifteenth century with the spiritual teachings of Guru Nanak.

[10] A Muslim human rights activist who advocated for Black empowerment and preached Islam in Black areas.

in the West, be it the US or Europe, to become Muslim. This was especially true with many imports from the US to the UK in terms of music and films.

I saw that the Nation of Islam were reconnecting with their roots, and I could understand the attraction the group had and why the number of members was constantly rising. It made sense to me. Something about it all was uniting Black people. I was going through a stage where I was becoming aware of the vernacular and felt excited to be swept along in the new cultural wave of awareness.

However, this was not the turning point to Islam for me. Even when the film *Malcolm X* came out in the cinemas, I didn't watch the film straightaway. I wasn't aware of Malcolm X's transition from the Nation of Islam to Sunni[11] Islam. I hadn't looked deeply into his life at that point. It was just a very Black conscious era[12] to be Muslim. It was in the air – Black pride was bubbling and was instilled in youth like me after years of not being aware of our predecessors' contributions to society. Many people were adopting Muslim names and entering Islam; it was an exhilarating moment. It was fresh, it was new and it offered hope, something to look forward to.

With all this around me, I couldn't not be into my culture, and on a random occasion I started watching the series adaptation of *Roots* written by Alex Hailey. It was on videotape, and I put the cassette in the player and pressed play. As I watched it, the surreal moment came when the main character Kunta Kinte was aboard the ship leaving his homeland, the Gambia, for the Atlantic Ocean and beyond.

Although I was certain I had seen that scene a number of times before, what I hadn't previously noticed was that while he was on the ship, he started calling out to his Lord 'Allah, please

---

[11] They recognise the first four caliphs as the Prophet Muhammad's rightful successors, whereas Shia Muslims believe that Muslim leadership belonged to Muhammad's son-in-law Ali and his descendants alone.

[12] Bringing to light the unfair treatment of Black people by systemic racism.

help me! Please help me, Allah, I am in trouble!' I suddenly realised, he was clearly making dua on the ship and I thought, 'Wow this was interesting! This was a man from West Africa who was going to the Americas; he was in a difficult situation, and he was a Muslim.'

This shifted my attention to think of *my* ancestors who had been in the same predicament as Kunta Kinte all those years ago, and I just sat in amazement as I connected the dots. My ancestors were most likely Muslims as well or at the very least, some of them were! I immediately felt a warm feeling – that I was in some way part of the global community of Muslims.

From then on, I was emotionally invested in Islam, and I wanted to find out more. From a cultural perspective, I was very interested in Islam just to see what it was made of, and I noticed that there were many similarities with Christianity.

In Christianity, there are grey areas where there is a lack of depth, such as in matters relating to Jesus. In one breath, I was told he was the son of God and then in another was told he was God himself. That was confusing.

These were contradictions I knew were there, but I hadn't delved further into them because I didn't want to ruffle any feathers or cause any waves. However, Islam clearly states that Jesus is not God nor does God have a son. Rather, Jesus is a prophet. That's when everything just clicked and made sense to me. He was a prophet of virgin birth, and he came with miracles of his time. That was a relief and sat more comfortably with me. Therefore, the transition to Islam was quite an easy one for me to make. Learning about Muhammad (pbuh) and how he fitted into this whole equation made perfect sense and so it was quite easy for me to take my shahadah.

When I took my shahadah, I was assisted by a friend who was a famous singer from around the area, his name was UK Apache.[13] Everyone knew him. He had a hit out at the time called 'The

---

[13] Abdul Wahab, a half–South African artist born and raised in London, more accepted by London's black community.

Original Nutter'. He was someone I used to see around and would say hello to in passing, but we had had no deep conversations before.

On one occasion, however, I turned the corner as I normally did, and there he was. I said, 'Hello', and he replied 'Hello', but this time he stopped me in my tracks and asked, 'What are you doing?' I responded, 'Nothing much'. I was just a sixteen-year-old at the time after all. Then he said something that was very strange and bizarre, but because I was on my journey of discovery, I saw it as a sign. He asked me, 'Do you want to come to the mosque?' and I replied excitedly, 'Yeah... of course I want to come to the mosque, I have actually been looking into this'. I felt moved, it was a clear sign from Allah.

I went to the mosque with him, and as I stepped inside, I felt something surreal. It was a very tranquil place. I felt at peace as I sat and watched people supplicating, prostrating and praying. I was quite affected by what I saw. It was an inner peace that caught me by surprise because I had never felt that way when I attended church.

Following that first experience at the mosque, I went along with him on random occasions a few more times. Then one day, he patiently pointed out that I had been coming to the mosque, making wudu,[14] praying with him and so on for a little while, so did I want to become Muslim? My answer was ambiguous. So he asked me a few more times, and I eventually said yes, I was ready to become a Muslim. When I had any questions, I approached him, and he quoted a hadith[15] with the answers, which I found good and thorough.

Once I took my shahadah, my transition to a full Muslim identity came gradually. I didn't start praying five times a day straight away. I prayed once a day, then twice for a while, and I let it slowly increase until I was comfortable praying five times a

---

[14] Cleansing parts of the body before the Islamic ritual prayer.

[15] Saying or tradition of Prophet Muhammad, accepted as a source of religious law and moral guidance.

day. Then after a whole week of praying five times a day, that was it, there was no turning back; it had become part of my life. I was quite young at the time and have grown up with Islam as my philosophy and moral compass. Now that I have spent most of my life as a Muslim, it's almost as though I was born into it.

During my teenage years, I had to part from a lot of people due to conflicts in our respective lifestyles. I tried to live by what I thought was the middle way, hanging around with my friends, going to pray at the mosque and then meeting up with them again, but it proved challenging. There came a point where I had to make a definite decision to really depart from influences around me that weren't serving me in who I wanted to become. I knew I was responsible for the choices I made as a young Muslim man.

I had no pressure on me when I became a Muslim, but there was some resistance from family members who didn't understand the religion. They thought it was quite alien to them and they had the same preconceived ideas I had when growing up – the fear of adopting someone else's culture and wanting to become Asian. At the beginning of my journey, it's true there was a lot of Asian influence. I used to wear Asian suits, thinking that was Islam, and say certain words thinking it was from Islam, for example 'namaz'.[16]

Ultimately, people showed me what they thought Islam was, and nothing was thrust upon me. People shared with me what Islam meant to them, as seen through their lens, and I appreciated that. I later realised I could comfortably be a Jamaican Muslim on par with any Arab or Asian Muslim. After the incident on 11 September 2001,[17] a few relatives did ask me about the religion I was in, a religion where people flew planes into buildings! I was cautioned to re-evaluate my life and the choices I was making, but after a while, the dust had settled, and people realised there

---

[16] Persian term similar to the Hindi/Sanskrit greeting 'namaste', today refers to the Islamic prayer (salah).

[17] A terrorist attack carried out on the Twin Towers at the World Trade Center in New York City.

were differences between certain groups and people. These reactions required patience from both sides and this took time, and now everything is fine.

Knowing Islam is the truth kept me grounded because I had seen enough evidence and was therefore satisfied with what I knew of the religion. A lot of my prior beliefs were confirmed in a more refined way. For instance, understanding the position of Prophet Isa (as) gave me much certainty and reassurance that I was not associating partners with Allah by calling him the son of God, which is disliked as stated in the Qur'an. I felt like I had been given a good insight into what is the Truth.

In hindsight, one thing that I possibly wouldn't have done was change my name. I also would not encourage others to do so if it does not conflict with anything good. If you don't have a name that is associated with idol worship or any other religion, then your name is fine; good names are good names. Obviously, I like my name, and I love the man it represents, and it is a complete honour to bear it, but nowadays when people become Muslim and I am present, I always let them know that they don't have to change their name if they don't want to. You can remain who you are.

Prophetic Tradition

'Give glad tidings and do not scare people away. Make things easy; do not make things difficult.' (Sahih Bukhari)

Supplication/Affirmation

Oh the Most High, I choose where to devote my energy.

4

Community holds you

'You are the best nation produced as an example for humankind. You enjoin what is right and forbid what is wrong and believe in Allah.' (3 Ali Imran:110)

For many people who seek to embrace Islam, it's all about finding and being with the right people, a community who reminds you of Allah. When you learn first-hand about yourself, where you are and where you're going, this leads to firmness, like roots reaching deep beneath you, stabilising you. This is Umar's story.

Unconsciously, I had always been on a path of faith, due to my family, friends and community. My parents and grandparents have Caribbean roots and were Christians, and the only Muslim I knew was a cousin in Trinidad. I wasn't aware of different religions growing up, but this changed when I started secondary school, where I encountered and was influenced by more communities. A lot of the people around me were into hip-hop music,[18] and through the lyrics, I was exposed to a plethora of messages of self-determination, interdependence and Black pride.

---

[18] Originated in the economically oppressed African American sections of the Bronx in New York City in the late 1970s as a means of self-expression, knowledge of self and consciousness.

My awakening to Islam and seeing its connection with Africa was through one of my neighbours, who was from Guyana and married a Senegalese man. She was pro-African, and her outlook on life matched that philosophy. Her husband, in his limited English, would proudly affirm the fact that they were all Muslims in Senegal. This was a moment of enlightenment.

I soon discovered that Africa had a sizeable Muslim population, and this sparked my interest further. I wanted to know what Islam looked like in Africa, and more importantly, how this came about. My search led me to gather many books on Islam in Africa and resulted in amazing discoveries like *The Caliph's Sister*, by Jean Boyd, which explains the life and legacy of Nana Asma'u, the great scholar, poet and daughter of Sheikh Uthman Dan Fodio of the Sokoto Caliphate in Northern Nigeria.

My uncle, who was a teacher (bless his soul), was also very eager for a youngster like me to have knowledge of my roots and my identity as a Black child growing up in the UK. In my teenage years, his influence and demeanour fuelled my curiosity – I began to see Muslims as a people with a history. I was aware then, but at that point, I was still focused on many things typical of youngsters my age. Islam as a religion wasn't something I felt seriously about practising, because as a teenager, discipline wasn't one of my strengths, and I understood discipline would be needed to follow Islam properly.

Because I wasn't necessarily looking for Islam, I thought my knowledge of it just kept me well-informed as a person who appreciated culture and history. However, during my secondary school years, there was a definite shift in my mindset and my relationship with the deen of Islam because by the age of nineteen, I had taken my shahadah!

My secondary school days were my awakening to Islam and where my spiritual journey began. My parents were well-embedded in their Christian roots and from the Caribbean. It was woven into our culture and our history to understand how we ended up on the island of Trinidad. However, growing up in the UK, I often went back to Trinidad for holidays and that was when I discovered I had a Muslim cousin and that my family is really quite racially mixed, particularly on my father's side. I saw African and Asian connections with lots of mixed marriages, but as a child, I didn't really notice the nuances, though I do recall my cousin once taking me to a mosque.

When I began secondary school, a myriad of events occurred, culminating in my classmates and I rebelling against the Catholic church. We questioned why Jesus was white, and none of us were satisfied with the responses. On the other side of the equation, Rastafari had put the scriptures into different contexts and linked things back to Africa. My uncle, who had taught in Nigeria during the 1970s, had seen Islam in context there, so he often talked to us about identifying with Africa.

By the 1980s, hip-hop was my music genre of choice, as its influence prevailed in the inner cities. Rap was used as a tool of expression for powerful messages and emotions, and it really captured the social realities of Black people and other marginalised groups. Interestingly, Islamic philosophy was intertwined in the hip-hop music I listened to. All this increased my awareness of who I was and from a social perspective, where I stood.

I also often listened to the news, where I heard about political aspects of Islam and realised it wasn't always held in a positive light. Though I was sixteen years old and not serious about making a commitment to Islam, I admired some famous Muslim personalities, such as Muhammad Ali and Malcolm X. However, knowing discipline was not my strong point, I thought that following it and praying five times a day could wait till later in my life, if at all.

At the age of eighteen, I was very comfortable in life, achieving academically, growing up as a teenager in London and experiencing typical social pleasures. Then I met a Muslim man at my sixth form college, a Black guy called Saeed, who had a strong political and religious presence. I felt drawn to listen to the way he spoke about Islam at the college's Islamic society. I was inspired by what I heard.

After this, a lot happened in my personal life that led me to ask a lot of questions. Then a few more Muslim brothers approached me and introduced me to brotherhood in Islam, where I felt a sense of calm and contentment. Shortly afterwards, I became a Muslim. I then found my local mosque, which has been the centre point of my Islamic affairs ever since.

It was a struggle to practise Islam for the first four years; it was emotional to give up my girlfriend and pray five times a day, but I knew I was doing it all for a higher purpose. During the holy month of Ramadan, I gave up certain desires. I broke off relationships, and my girlfriend at the time wasn't pleased about it, but I wasn't naïve of the responsibilities of marriage as a youngster. My biggest mantra was 'know thyself'. I wasn't into drinking or drugs. Through my transition from boyhood to manhood, I examined my relationships and navigated my way through life, and I feel that accepting my decisions made me stronger as an individual.

I attended the university ISoc[19] and the African Caribbean society meetings at my campus, both of which shaped my ideas. I was interested in the religion and in my people. I made sure I was not only spending time with Muslims; I was hanging out with my own community and other people who I thought it fine to mix with.

After graduating from university, I travelled to Senegambia, West Africa. This was the climax of my spiritual journey. My neighbour had often invited me, so when I eventually agreed, it turned out to be the journey of a lifetime. That trip will always remain one of the sweetest experiences of my life; I really felt like I was home. As my parents' youngest child (and the only one who grew up in London), I was able to discover myself in my own way. I was given a lot of freedom, which enabled me to be myself.

I didn't face any resistance from my mother or father when I took my shahadah, but I did from other relatives. My family

---

[19] An Islamic society present at universities in the UK.

respected discipline, but they were not going to let me be an idiot or an extremist. My father put me through my paces because of the media slant on Islam, and others were a bit wary. They all had their questions for me, and quite frankly, I couldn't answer many of them at the time. However, they could sense that my intentions and feelings were genuine, and fortunately, I had good friends around me. My parents always looked at my friends to know who I was becoming.

My parents wouldn't allow me to distance myself from them just because I chose to follow a faith different to theirs. On the Muslim platform, there were persuasions of Islam entering the stratosphere, and sometimes things did get heated and strict. I loved my music which was part of my identity, nonetheless there were some other things I had to let go of. I heard about musicians such as Yusuf Islam.[20] So I had to navigate my love of music and carnival.

As my journey in the deen unfolded, I did get a bit confused with my identity and what was expected of me, so some did take advantage of my newness. It was all a bit of a learning curve, and I have no regrets. I had a good network of friends who would tell me if they were concerned about me. My barometer was not just my Muslim friends; my non-Muslim friends could freely tell me if they were concerned that I was overindulging in one area and not keeping it balanced.

I addressed my inner self to examine myself, and I became a Muslim who embraced tasawwuf.[21] This led me to see my brothers as mirrors to myself. Looking back, my uncle often said 'Don't hurry the curry,' and I admit I was hasty in many decisions I made as a youth. With a bit more patience I would have eased my way into situations, but Allah is always Karim[22] with His slaves.

---

[20] Formerly known as artist Cat Stevens.

[21] Islamic spirituality and purification of the soul.

[22] Most generous.

Prophetic Tradition

'Whoever does a lot of istighfar (asking for forgiveness), Allah will provide him a way out of each concern he has, and will solve all his troubles, and will provide him with livelihood from sources that were not known to him.' (Ahmad)

Supplication/Affirmation

Ya Allah, O Opener, I call on You whenever I need guidance.

5

You still on that Muslim 'ting?

*'Indeed, those who have said, "Our Lord is Allah" and
then remain on a right course – the angels will descend
upon them, saying "Do not fear and do not grieve but
receive good tidings of Paradise which you were
promised."' (41 Fussilat:30)*

IT takes a lot to make a 180-degree turn in your life. We are
all born with a moral compass, and it takes considerable
willpower to follow that despite everything else vibrating on a
different frequency. However, with Allah all is possible. This is
Rakin's story.

In the 1950s and then again in the 1990s, the Nigerian
community arrived in Britain in numbers to pursue economic
opportunities following economic failures by the government
due to a combination of factors. One of the Nigerian families
who arrived in the UK was mine. My father was Muslim, and my
mother was Christian. Growing up, I wasn't familiar with the
religion of Islam. I knew I had a Muslim name, and I was Muslim,
but beyond that, my understanding of the deen was hazy. I
started contemplating God from the age of seventeen and by
twenty, I was practising Islam.

To begin with, some friends and I were part of a conscious hip-hop group called Cash Crew.[23] We took a political stance and wrote lyrics on social issues. Our record company had to market us differently because we weren't like the artists they usually signed. They suggested we perform our tracks at Speakers' Corner[24] in Hyde Park because there were a mix of open-minded listeners there, and most were seekers.

Every Sunday, we shared our lyrics and then went round listening to other speakers. Two speakers caught our attention every time, one was called Imam Nurideen and the other was Mohammed Kadjar. Both were articulate and inspiring; they clearly attracted the crowds and were by far the best orators in the park. On one occasion, we were listening to one of them, and a man called Hassan Eid approached us. He asked, 'Would you like to learn more about what they're talking about?,' and we replied 'Yes, sure.' So he invited us to his house, which is a customary Islamic practice when inviting people to Islam. This was the beginning of our journey to Islam.

Prior to this meeting, I felt deflated. I had been reflecting on my life because while I was in the group, we performed and partied a lot, and I knew something was amiss. One day, we sat down honestly and thought there must be more to life than this, just doing the same old thing day in and day out. The more we opened up and expressed our feelings, the more we agreed with one another and were convinced there had to be more. This yearning was the seed that put us on the quest to Islam. Our only intention was to find the truth and live by it.

With this inclination towards the truth, we all eventually took the shahadah with Hassan Eid. He was a friendly Tanzanian man who opened his doors to let us spend a lot of time at his house. He patiently supported our transition to practising Islam, and he taught us the fundamentals – the five pillars of Islam. During

---

[23] A UK rap group in Ladbroke Grove in the mid 1980s.

[24] A traditional site for public speeches and debates since the mid-1800s, which ended in 2008 with the rise in social media, diminishing its cultural value.

this time, he was our mentor, and his home was akin to our Dar al-Arqam.[25] We also learnt about the strong connection Islam had with Africa and great African Muslim leaders like Sheikh Uthman Dan Fodio (ra).[26]

We marvelled that one of the first universities in the world was built in Timbuktu in Mali, a landlocked country in West Africa. We also discovered that Mansa Musa (ra), also from Mali, was the richest man to ever live. This heightened our appreciation and brought to light that Islam and Africa have an interwoven relationship – there is no separating the two.

As I started taking Islam seriously, I realised I was adopting a way of life, not just a set of religious rituals. I realised there were lots of things in my life that were counterproductive and had to be dropped to fit into what Allah says in the Holy Qur'an and the Sunnah[27] of our beloved Prophet (pbuh). However, I didn't dismantle my life abruptly. I just built a new life consisting of the Qur'an and Sunnah, and, eventually, my old life meant nothing to me.

When news that our crew had become Muslim spread around our area, some couldn't believe we really had changed. After a while, when they saw that we really were focused on practising the religion, they respected us for the effort required to adhere to the faith wholeheartedly. At first, we found it quite easy due to the excitement. This pushed us forward to become the best Muslims we could be.

We soon realised the many health benefits to practising Islam as well as the peace in our hearts, minds and bodies. We hadn't expected this. We had never experienced anything before like the peace that is found in the Muslim prayer prostration. We also benefited from the discipline. The prayers have rules and

---

[25] The first house where the Muslims studied and took refuge.

[26] A Fulani scholar, religious teacher, revolutionary and philosopher who founded the Sokoto Caliphate in 1804.

[27] Traditions and practices of Prophet Muhammad, the model who Muslims follow.

regulations, set at distinct times of the day. The ritual preparation to pray to Allah helps our focus. We saw that when we were disciplined in one area of our lives, we found it was easier to transfer that momentum of discipline to other areas of our lives too.

With regards to health, a lifestyle of drinking alcohol, smoking and taking drugs is harmful (haram)[28] to the body, so all of that is pushed aside to keep the body pure. With a pure mind, you have a chance to work on yourself, on self-development, on improving and controlling your emotions and thinking about where you are, where you want to go and what you want to achieve. You also have the opportunity to commit to your family and community. On the whole, Islam definitely made me a better human being, someone much healthier, focused and happier than I would have been, but this only happens when following the Qur'an and the last Prophet (pbuh). Put in the practice, and you will be able to achieve your goals inshallah.[29]

In the early days of practising this religion, a lot of people that I grew up with thought we weren't going to be able to take this religion seriously. Many thought we would just drop off and go back to our old habits of partying. The question that we were asked a lot and eventually turned into a joke afterwards was 'Yo man, you still Muslim?' We were asked every few months, 'You lot still on that Muslim 'ting?' The lack of faith they had in us to commit to Islam was quite sad.

One of my teachers later taught me that one of the best things a person can have are friends who support you, make things easier for you and want you to better your life by believing wholeheartedly in you. Prophet Muhammad (pbuh) had this in his beloved wife Khadijah (ra) and his beloved companion Abu Bakr as-Siddiq (ra).

I would not have changed a thing because the powerful thing about a journey is that you reach a stage, look back and only

---

[28] Forbidden by Islamic law.
[29] God willing.

appreciate how far you have come. Furthermore, there is certain knowledge that I learnt and only later could I use those experiences and social skills. All my experiences have brought me to the position I am in now. My past experiences mean that I can talk to people who are on this journey, help and guide them on how to move forward and how to stay strong.

My journey has been an exciting one; it has made me truly appreciate the blessings in Islam, including the cleanliness, physical and spiritual. By keeping my body and mind away from anything evil, following the Qur'an and Sunnah has proved to be extremely positive as it continues to benefit me emotionally and mentally.

Prophetic Tradition

'By Allah, were Allah to guide a single man through you would be better for you than a herd of red camels.' (Sahih Bukhari)

Supplication/Affirmation

O Allah, You are Peace. Peace comes from You. I take responsibility for my life.

6

Paradise lies under the feet of your mother

'And your Lord has decreed that you not worship except Him, and to parents, good treatment. Whether one or both of them reach old age [while] with you, say not to them "uff" and do not repel them but speak to them a noble word.' (17 al-Isra:23)

One of the biggest obstacles to following a path different to the one you were brought up in is meeting the disapproval of your kin, in particular your parents. However, when they follow you into the deen, that's one of the sweetest gifts. This is Abdul Ahad's story.

One of my cousins became a Muslim quite a few years ahead of me. He often held religious meetings at his house. At one of the meetings, he showed a video of Louis Farrakhan[30] giving a talk, which I watched intently. He talked about Islam and nothing else and this sparked my interest in the deen.

I was in my room one night, when I just got up and went to my mother and told her I wanted to go to the mosque. She didn't question me or try to stop me. I left and headed to the only mosque I knew at the time, which wasn't far from home. When

---

[30] An American religious man who is the leader of the Nation of Islam.

I arrived, I enquired about Islam from the first people I met inside: what was it and how to practise it. They gave me some explanations, da'wah[31] and also some books. Grateful, I took them home and began to read.

Upon entering the mosque that first time, I remember I felt completely at peace, and I could see Islam as a very clean religion (e.g., making ablution, its symbolism and the purity of it all). Due to my mature age and awareness of myself, I was able to pace myself comfortably, even in the early days of my journey towards Islam. I knew I didn't need to please anyone but my Creator, so there was no pressure from outside forces. I just did what felt right to me and moved on regardless of what might have been going on around me. I was able to shut out the noise.

Around three months later, I met a brother who said to me (among other things) that if I wanted to become a Muslim, I shouldn't waste time because I could pass away at any time. He suggested I take my shahadah. I agreed that I had nothing holding me back from doing this. Not long after that encounter, I did take my shahadah at the mosque. I saw the same brother on and off for a while and he was always helpful.

I am quite a calm person, so when I took my shahadah, I took my time getting used to the various rituals practised in Islam. I didn't find things difficult at all because I didn't try to rush anything or push myself. I stayed in my own lane, so I felt no pressure. I went into it all with my eyes completely open.

I did tell my mother straight away, and she was okay with it. She had always been quite religious herself, and she trusted me enough with the spirituality of Islam that she also took her shahadah a short time after me! I didn't need to convince her it was the truth. She saw it herself. She may have taken her shahadah due to what she saw in me and my behaviour; I don't know. However, I always had a close relationship with her, so it was pleasing that we could share the journey in the *deen* together.

---

[31] The act of calling people to embrace Islam.

I grew attached to the mosque; being there and praying in congregation really felt like home to me. It gave me a sense of purpose and identity, knowing where I ought to be at certain times of the day. When I know I am in the right place at the right time, it does wonders for my sense of self. Right up till today it helps a lot. Even while telling this story, I am here at the mosque. It's the best place I could ever be. One of the groups of people who will be shaded on the day that there is no shade but Allah's shade are those whose hearts are attached to the mosque. I hope to be one of them.

When I took my shahadah, there were a few Afro-Caribbean Muslims around in South London, so it was nice that there was support. There may not have been a lot in numbers, but they were there, and their presence was felt. Nowadays, it's not the same as it was. Everyone is a bit scattered across the country, and the community doesn't seem to be as close as it used to be. I don't know why.

People seem to have changed; it could just be the times we are living in. In the early days of my Islam, people would meet up a lot more regularly, and you could feel a real sense of togetherness. However, at the mosque, I can always feel a sense of community even if it may not be apparent when I step outside of it.

Prophetic Tradition

'Whenever someone goes to the mosque in the morning or evening, Allah prepares for him a place in Paradise.' (Sahih Muslim)

Supplication/Affirmation

O Allah, Lord of the people! Whenever I feel overwhelmed, I keep it simple.

7

When one door shuts…

'Perhaps you hate a thing and it is good for you, and perhaps you love a thing and it is bad for you. And Allah knows, while you know not.' (2 al-Baqarah:216)

WE often assume we know what is best for us; we observe, study and ask those we trust around us. However, when things happen that we don't expect, our immediate response to it can change the trajectory of our lives forever. This is Iman's story.

I have always believed in God. I remember when I was a child, I would climb into my parents' bed and cry, because I didn't understand why they didn't believe and I did. They tried to console me, but it didn't change their agnostic views, and I found it hard to put my disappointment into words. So I grew up with my own natural predisposition to the Creator; my home did not acknowledge or encourage a connection with God.

Years later, while he was still only a baby, my son died. No one prepares you for that sort of grief, so afterwards, I decided to start attending church. My neighbours were extremely religious, almost Mormon[32] like, but my ex-husband, my son's father, didn't believe in God. He believed in science. This troubled me, and I confided in my priest that it didn't feel right coming to

---

[32] A religious and cultural group of the Latter-day Saints movement started by Joseph Smith in the 1820s.

church and then returning home to a man who didn't believe in God. The priest didn't tell me to leave my son's father, but when I found Islam, I understood why it was counterproductive to marry a non-Muslim. It is very difficult for a couple to grow when one partner is headed in a polar opposite direction to the other in terms of interests.

Although I wasn't looking for another religion per se at that moment, my friend and I often talked about God and religion, and I always believed in a Higher Being, so much so that whenever I went out at night, I would say a little prayer, 'Please God, don't let me die until I find the Truth,' even though I didn't know where to look for this Truth.

After I separated from my husband, I worked in Nottingham, where I regularly popped into a local coffee shop run by a Tunisian man and his English wife. They served great coffee! I would place my usual order, and when he brought it over, the owner often spoke to me about religion, and I found it so interesting. At the same time, I found it bizarre because, in spite of all the Pakistanis I knew (who I sort of knew were Muslim), I thought only Christians believed in God.

I had no idea that other people outside of the fold of Christianity believed in God too. He told me a lot about the religion of Islam, and he gave me a book by Ahmad Deedat[33] titled *Who Moved the Stone?* I accepted the book gratefully and took it home to read. After reading that book, I was stunned, and I thought to myself 'Oh my God, this is the truth!'

I felt excited and elated at the same time, and I wanted to know more about it straightaway, but then I got a reality check when I remembered, 'Oh dear, I've hired a car to go to the London Nottinghill Carnival[34] with my mates this weekend.' I thought to myself that I ought to stick to my plans, and I didn't

---

[33] Muslim author and orator on comparative religion who held inter-religious debates with Christians.

[34] An annual Caribbean festival that has been taking place on the streets of Notting Hill area since 1966.

want to let my mates down. We did go to the carnival; we raved and had a great time, but all the while at the back of my mind I couldn't get thoughts of Islam out of my head.

When I arrived back in Nottingham, I felt a bit embarrassed to see the coffee shop owner, because I had had such a good time I didn't want him to see me. From what he had already explained to me, I believed I was on a path of self-discovery to connect with God, and I didn't think my partying was really aligned with that.

Not long afterwards, he stopped me at the petrol station and gestured to come have some coffee. I went back over to the coffee shop where after all was said and done, he wanted to make sure in front of Allah that he had done right by me. He had fulfilled his responsibility and told me everything that I needed to know about Islam. He asked if I understood what he had been saying; I agreed I had. So then he asked if I believed in God, and I responded I did. Then, as I got up to leave, he asked me, if I walked out that door now and got knocked over, what did I think my fate would be? Well, that cleared up any confusion or hesitation I had at that moment and put everything into crystal clear perspective. With these thoughts, I said, 'Tell me what to do; I'm going to be a Muslim.'

I came back over from the door and took my shahadah that day. It was an amazing idea that I had to change my name; I realised later on that it wasn't a necessity. They gave me a choice of names, and they said one of them was Fatima but at the time I didn't know the significance of Sayyidah Fatima, (ra) and I felt I'm already fat! I loved Iman, and they said it meant faith. That was nice because I believed I had faith.

I went home to my children that day still on cloud nine; they were all fully aware of my interest in Islam. It was no secret; I had occasionally taken them with me to the coffee shop too. I felt I had always been naïve as a child, but my children were so discerning. Nothing got past them, and they understood totally.

For the past two years we had also stopped celebrating Christmas; I explained to them I felt it was ridiculous to celebrate it. It would be better to give to people who didn't have anything rather than to kids who just leave it outside or throw it away after a short while. They had observed this change in me already, so when I said to them 'Guess what? I'm a Muslim!' I wasn't sure what to expect, but it wasn't a chorus of wailing from either end of the bunk beds! I asked them all what was wrong. Between sobs they responded, 'We're not going to have any more birthday parties!'

Unbeknownst to me, they had worked out what I was up to. They had found out about Islam too on their own. They had already discovered that Muslims didn't celebrate birthdays and with us not celebrating Christmas either, emotions were high. My son's birthday was coming up, and I reassured them we would celebrate it. Interestingly, my children's prime concern about Islam was not being able to celebrate birthdays anymore.

A few days later, I was still so excited, and I really felt the need to tell somebody else that I was Muslim. I met up in town with a lady I knew and spent one to two hours telling her that I was a Muslim now and what it meant for me. I couldn't go to the pub anymore and I couldn't do this and that, and she just accepted everything I said without judgement.

Shortly afterwards she told me she had to go up the road and would I like to go with her? I said sure, no problem. I walked along beside her only to realise she expected me to go into a pub with her. I looked at her incredulously and said, 'I just explained to you I can't go in a pub anymore.' She was confused. That's when it dawned on me that I had told her all those things in theory, but to look at me you wouldn't know I was any different. I looked the same. That night I went home and reflected on that. I woke up the next day ready to put a hijab on my head.

At the van hire company where I worked, I often read an English translation of the Qur'an, and my boss noticed and jokingly would say to me, 'I hope you're not getting any ideas. I hope you're not thinking about doing anything with all that reading.' So unsurprisingly, when I turned up at work with a scarf on ready to serve those requesting van hire, he fussed over that and said I couldn't sit there with my scarf on. When I gently protested it was only a piece of cloth, he asked if I could compromise by taking it off while at work and putting it back on when I went home. I told him that would be pointless.

Not only did my cheeks start to feel flushed, but my whole body was burning up. I recalled the strength it took to muster up the courage to get on the bus to get to work. In my head, it was as though everyone was watching me. Anyway, he was adamant. I couldn't sit there as a customer sales rep with my scarf on. He repeated that I would have to take it off and put it on when I went home. I said sorry, I couldn't do that and left.

I then boarded a bus which went through the town and into the market. Still sweating from the job situation, I got off and soon bumped into two of my friends who both exclaimed 'Oh Linda, you look so beautiful!' That was all the validation I needed. I immediately relaxed and walked around the town centre with them for a bit. When I got to the market, I saw the man who had been instrumental in my becoming a Muslim, and he said, 'Do you want a job in the market?' I smiled in amazement.

By that same afternoon, I had a job in a market stall in front of many people. I couldn't hide wearing a scarf, and within an hour of being at the stall, a sister who was also a convert came over to me. It turned out we had many other things in common, so we had an instant connection and are still very good friends to this day. She was my first Muslim friend apart from the man and his wife who told me about Islam in the first place.

When I told my mum I had embraced Islam, the first thing she asked me was did I know that Muslims could marry more than one wife? I responded, 'Well, that's a brilliant idea!' I remember when it came to light that my husband had had an affair, I told him I wish I knew of a religion where he could marry more than one wife because I would tell him to marry her. He told me she always beautified herself with makeup, and so I told him to live with her for a week. However, by the next day I got a call from him asking if I had cooked. I said, 'Doesn't she cook?' He responded that she didn't. He had to think about that. I also told my mum that it saves men having half a dozen girlfriends.

At least the men have to think about their commitment to them. My responses to her didn't go down too well of course, and she replied that she knew more about Muslims than I would ever know. At that time, her statement didn't mean much to me, but years later after my mum passed, it turned out she was Jewish. I then understood where she was coming from, considering the relationship between Jews and Arab Muslims.

As a new Muslim, I assimilated straight away into a lovely community in Nottingham. I felt so fortunate; it was such a lovely time, and there was a beautiful atmosphere when the women gathered together every Friday. I had a strong community where my children were accepted by all; it felt incredible. I had always believed in God, and as soon as I became Muslim, everything fell effortlessly into place for me.

I had never believed that Jesus was the son of God, and the idea that Jesus died for us was confusing because that implied that we could all sin as much as we wanted, because we were going to be forgiven anyway. That just didn't make sense to me. I was informed that according to the Islamic tradition, my son who died at six weeks old will be calling me in Jannah.[35] As I went through the different stages of grief with this new understanding, I consoled myself that at least he didn't die in an accident or in a difficult situation and that there was a reason behind it. And that eased my heart.

Later on, I moved to London, where I met many types of Muslims, and things started to change for me as I had to adjust to the differences around me. The first time I went to Hyde Park Corner, I learnt there were seventy-three sects[36] in Islam. Later that day, I phoned a friend and anxiously asked how I would know I was in the right one! I heard so many conversations in that park it made my head spin.

I felt I met every single sect in the park, so it was a worry at

---

[35] According to Islam, it is Paradise, the final abode for the righteous.
[36] Different schools of Islamic thought with differing branches of understanding the religion.

first because I intentionally became a Muslim, and so I wanted to get it right. I also worried about my children; my youngest was four years old at the time. Of course, I didn't want to bombard them with information, but at the same time, I valued certain things. For example, I was conscious of what we let into our minds, so we didn't watch much TV. This was the case even before I was a Muslim.

I wanted to give my children a strong foundation and allow them to make their own choices as they grew. Presently, I have fifteen grandchildren, and some of them understand basic morals, the dangers out there and the need to protect themselves by not doing certain things, and they also know about things I do. One of my grandchildren informed his teacher at school that Muhammad (pbuh) is the last and final prophet and there is only one God; they are brave children today.

My journey has been a wonderful one. I have never looked back. I have met many different people on my journey, and what I have realised is it is not about what you say, it is about what you do. I know sometimes people want to push Islam down your throat, but it's not the right approach. It's all about your actions; people see who you really are through your actions.

Prophetic Tradition

Allah said in a well-known Hadith Qudsi, 'I am as my servant thinks [expects] I am. I am with him when he mentions Me. If he mentions Me to himself, I mention him to Myself, and if he mentions Me in an assembly, I mention Him in an assembly greater than it. If he draws near to Me a hand's length, I draw near to him an arm's length. And if he comes to Me walking, I go to him at speed.'

Supplication/Affirmation

Allah is sufficient for me. I remember that my life purpose is to worship Allah.

8

Motherhood

'Indeed, those who believe and do good, the Most Merciful
will certainly bless them with genuine love.'
(19 Maryam:96)

Pain and confusion can bring about clarity. Sometimes a search for meaning can lead one to find their path, or their calling. What we yearn for, we will see, and as our lens focuses, we affect our own reality. This is Amina's story.

I was born into a Christian family who were not very practicing. They did go to church, but only occasionally. Nonetheless, they believed in God irrefutably. When I was younger, the trinity and some other fundamental Christian beliefs were confusing and just didn't make sense to me. I set out to find a church that was good for me, and although I tried, that didn't happen.

When I was eighteen, I started to learn about the Black struggle: the suffering that led to the civil rights movement and the pain experienced by Africans across the diaspora. I really respected Malcolm X and his intentions; however, I didn't feel the need to become a Muslim because I believed I wasn't that bad of a person or that I needed such a big change in my life. Having said that, I loved what Islam did for Malcolm X. I felt it was important to attend meetings and talks that spoke on the Black plight. Later, I met people from the Nation of Islam and other Black groups, one of whom handed me a book by Ahmad Thomson called *The Dajjal: The Antichrist*. I was still sceptical of the need for a paradigm shift in my life, but I chose to remain open-minded and took the book. After reading that book, things started to change for me internally and I thought perhaps Islam *was* the way.

Something really strange happened to me on my journey. A spiritual woman told me that I would, within two months, meet the man I would settle down with and I would get a strong religious framework. She even told me that the person would be born in January or February and that I should go home and pray for guidance. I wasn't sure what to make of her message, but I did go home and pray. It turned out she was right. I met my husband-to-be two months later. And he was born in January.

When I think about it, I was quite disillusioned with Christianity and my lifestyle of partying and shallow living. It was uplifting and inspiring to listen to Malcolm X's speeches and see the efficiency of the Nation of Islam and other groups participating in Black people's struggles. I felt there was hope! My surety that I had identified the right path and my feeling that this was right for me was further reinforced and also solidified when I met my future husband.

When I met my future husband, I realised from his actions and the way he spoke that he wasn't in the Nation of Islam; he was an orthodox Muslim. I found this doctrine intriguing and interesting. I now had an emotional reason to look at this religion again, more seriously. I went with him to Speakers Corner in Hyde Park, where people would gather to debate heartfelt issues. From there, I realised that the Muslims always seemed to make more sense to me with their logical reasoning than the other religions. I also had a friend called Tracy, who was also moving away from Christianity, and we often met to sit together to discuss issues concerning women in Islam, and then we studied more aspects of the religion.

Very soon, I found myself defending Islam in conversations and decided that if I was defending it, then it must be something

I truly believed in. It would therefore be dishonourable to God if I then didn't live by it. So I decided to take my shahadah with a Tanzanian brother who had also taken my husband's shahadah. Shortly afterwards we got married. Alhamdulillah, Islam found me when I was twenty-one years old.

The idea of taking my shahadah appealed to me a lot, as I hoped to live a clean life, learning about God and practising Islam well. At the beginning of my life as a Muslim, I was obsessed and just revelled in wanting to read and read and read. However, after a while, I began to find it difficult, because I was soon to be a new mother, and with that, my life changed again dramatically, where I had to grow up to be a mum and wife and establish this new religion in my life.

When I got started, I excitedly crammed in trying to learn the prayers and the rules surrounding them. After that initial energetic stage and being in love with my new religion, the reality of being a new mum set in. I also began to feel the enormous responsibility of bringing a child into this world and being equipped to teach them this beautiful way of life ordained by Allah (swt).[37]

I felt confident that I had chosen the right path with Islam because I could see my way of life become much better and straightforward than before. There were no added pressures to do things I didn't always want to. As time passed, I knew it was the best decision I could have ever made.

The thought of returning to my old life was disturbing and out of the question, unless Allah allowed something to happen to my mental health. Alhamdulillah, what also helped was that I was blessed to have a husband who was a realistic Muslim, and we very early on met a sheikh. He was a father figure, a mentor called Sheikh Babikr who was a brilliant role model and guide for us as he portrayed a balanced life, adopting a middle path like the Prophet (pbuh).

---

[37] Subhana wa ta'ala, the Most Glorious, the Most High.

When I took my shahadah, my family showed slight reservations, but it was nothing compared to others. They all later respected the positive impact Islam had on us as a family. Unfortunately, I didn't try to stay close to the friends I had growing up. We became distant when I became Muslim. I felt I had outgrown them, and with my reluctance to join them in certain pursuits, they too realised that I wasn't the same girl anymore, and the gap between us widened. I was twenty-two then and still growing up myself and at the same time focusing on acclimatising to new territory, spiritually and emotionally. For sure, I found some things difficult, like the prayers that took me some time to establish properly, despite my enthusiasm. The unfamiliar words in Arabic tested my tongue a bit. However, I found that when you stick it out and don't give up, Allah gifts you with the will to do it consistently till it becomes part of you.

Prophetic Tradition

'Wondrous is the affair of the believer, for there is good for him in every matter and this is not the case with anyone except the believer. If he is happy, then he thanks Allah and thus there is good for him. If he is harmed, then he shows patience, and thus there is good for him.' (Sahih Muslim)

Supplication/Affirmation

Ya Wadud Ya Rahman, I hope in Allah's Mercy.

9

The trip of a lifetime

*'And when they hear what was revealed to the Messenger,
you see their eyes overflowing with tears because of what
they have recognised as the truth. They say, "Our Lord,
we have believed so count us among the witnesses."'*
(5 al-Maidah:83)

AN invitation is never taken lightly, and an invitation from Allah is an honour like no other. Many go on pilgrimage with great expectations; some believe all you need is to show up with sincerity and be present. This is Tzipporah's story.

When I first married my husband, I did not know what Islam was or even what I was doing for the first four years, until we moved to the UK and were around Muslims. One Ramadan, my husband spent the last ten nights at the mosque in 'itikaf.[38] We lived a short walking distance from the mosque, so as a gesture of friendliness, he offered to take another brother's clothes home to be washed as well. I washed both of their clothes, and this led to the brother wishing to meet me afterwards. He later introduced me to his wife, and we all became family friends. I

---

[38] An Islamic practice consisting of staying in the mosque for a period of time and devoting oneself to worship and staying away from worldly affairs.

soon met their friends and since I hadn't long been in the country, I tasted the wonderful spirit of sisterhood.

With the ebb and flow of life, I met more sisters and eventually I confided in a select few of them that I feared I should take my shahadah again, as in my first four years as a Muslim I lacked knowledge about the worship of Allah. But the sisters, full of love and compassion, helped me realise that one of the names of Allah is the All Merciful and that I was always a Muslim since I believed in Him and His Messenger ﷺ. They explained that our faith rises and falls. Their kind words soothed my heart and gave me the strength and conviction I needed to move forward and learn more of the religion without the mental block of guilt. This revived willingness enhanced my relationship with Allah, and my five daily prayers helped foster a connection with Allah.

This was the cornerstone of my new life and when I had my children, I then began to study the Islamic sciences through seminars, lectures and study circles. The pull for understanding was etched in my mind and as I sought knowledge, I started to realise my place in the grand scheme of things. I came to the unshakeable conclusion that Allah loved me.

As I grew in the faith, it became apparent to me that not everyone feels the same way all of the time. I tried to force a connection with Allah, like the one that I saw others demonstrate, but when I was copying others, I wasn't being true to myself, and I was resisting my true being in favour of something I saw outside of me. I realised all I had to do was follow the sunnah of the Prophet (pbuh), and this made me feel at ease.

Years later, the opportunity of a lifetime came up – a trip to Mecca for the lesser pilgrimage called 'umrah. I anticipated that this would bring about my true connection with Allah, whatever 'true' meant. However, my focus and observation of others clouded my own insight about what was taking place within me.

I was both excited and overwhelmed when I first set my eyes on the Kaaba.[39] I had heard of the fireworks and butterflies in the stomach, with tears flowing down cheeks, but that just didn't happen for me. These were the reactions I often heard and read about, so I naturally wondered if something was wrong with me. I wondered if I should fake the emotions to force them to the surface? Don't get me wrong – I wasn't unimpressed. I just assumed it would be an overwhelming epiphany, which it wasn't. After my initial physical response or lack thereof, I decided to stop my preoccupation with searching and just listen to myself for my own version of the sacred connection.

Although my resounding expectation wasn't realised, I gazed around precariously and listened and tried to feel in touch with my inner self. A special feeling didn't manifest itself while I was in front of the Kaaba, and that was okay. I then started to ponder: what does a connection with Allah really mean? I decided it couldn't be something that just happened in and of itself like a light switch, an isolated event that needed to be repeated again and again to get that same spiritual euphoria. In reality, I realised I connect with Allah in every moment of every single day. When I go through testing situations with my husband or children, I lose my composure and, at that moment, I do not remember my connection with Allah. But thankfully, Islam's emphasis on dhikr[40] is so key and paramount as a tool, so I use salawat[41] on the Prophet ﷺ as a means to recalibrate myself and, ultimately, connect with Allah.

Whenever I got busy or angry, I studied myself and I began to realise and know myself, my triggers and my preoccupations with the necessities of life. Then I deliberately began to do certain things that would reconnect me with Allah, be it every so

---

[39] A building at the centre of Islam's most important mosque, the Masjid al-Haram in Mecca. It is the most sacred site in Islam.

[40] A form of Islamic meditation in which phrases or prayers are repeatedly chanted to remember God.

[41] Salutations upon Prophet Muhammad ﷺ, also performed in the salah and whenever his name ﷺ is mentioned.

often, to interrupt my normal pattern of behaviour. Once, while praying, I found myself crying, not because I was sad, but out of appreciation for all that Allah does for me, and it dawned on me how important I am to Allah that He wrote this book, the Holy Qur'an, to me.

It was necessary for me to feel important. The feeling of individual acknowledgement and care from Allah made me weep a few Ramadans ago during the taraweeh[42] prayers. I didn't understand all that the imam was reciting in Arabic but when he reached the verse that spoke of 'the believing women and the believing men', I felt so honoured to be included in that category of the Qur'an, it made my heart smile to know I was getting a mention in the Qur'an.

I intentionally chose to understand that the believing women included me because I believe in Allah regardless of my shortcomings. I believe I have value and that Allah invited me to think along those lines and that of course He invited me to His house. My thoughts filtered how I read, perceived, analysed and understood the Quran. I strove to understand the words of Allah the best I could.

It was about realigning myself with the Qur'an because daily I fall short. I realise that whatever I put into my relationship with Allah is what I get out of it. For instance, the more I read a surah, the clearer it is to me, just like the hadith states, 'the ear you hear with is Him hearing for you.' So I felt so protected and honoured. But I would be lying if I say I'm connected a great deal. I'm not; it is like that with faith, it rises and falls, but what I love is that it's different for everyone and that is what makes it so special. It's really comforting because there isn't one size fits all; there isn't only one way of looking at things. We each have our lens. As long as I was honestly striving with myself, I felt calm. All things are open to anyone if they believe and are willing to try.

---

[42] Nightly prayers in Ramadan performed exclusively by Sunni Muslims, involving reading long portions of the Qur'an and performing many rakahs.

When it was time to leave Medina, I wanted to stay on but my time was up. All in all, the experiences and memories I took from Mecca and my 'umrah trip in general have helped foster a stronger connection with Allah. To be honest, I was really overwhelmed with the emotion of wanting to stay, which was when the tears flowed and my emotions were really heavy, but I had to leave to get absorbed back into the matrix of work and responsibilities. We part only to return in sha Allah.

Prophetic Tradition

'One 'umrah to the next is an expiation for whatever happened between them and the only reward for an accepted hajj is Paradise.' (Sahih Bukhari)

Supplication/Affirmation

O Turner of hearts, I turn to you.

10

A picture paints a thousand words

'Say, "I am only a man like you, to whom it has been revealed that your god is one God. So whoever would hope for the meeting with his Lord – let him do righteous work and not associate in the worship of his Lord anyone."' (18 al-Kahf:110)

Curiosity can take you places you never imagined. Children see the world through eyes of wonder. Experiencing Islam through a traditional framework with a natural rhythm can build an overall unstained worldview. This is Mustafa's story.

I grew up with my mother and grandmother, who used to take me on visits to the Gambia. I was continuously exposed to Islam there, as it is a Muslim majority country. I walked along its streets and saw people gathered in circles of dhikr (remembrance of Allah), and I heard the Qur'an being recited. I was very curious as a child and wanted to know what this religion was that some people were practising and, more importantly, why wasn't my family practising it? This drew me into my family history, where I discovered that my mother's family are from a group called the

Creole,[43] descendants from liberated African slaves who returned to Africa after the slave trade ended.

Some people who had been on slave ships en route to America and the Caribbean were freed by British anti-slavery patrols, and they resettled in Freetown, Sierra Leone. They then travelled to the Gambia and other places, and some went to Nigeria to trade. This is why my Gambian family have English surnames like Briggs, Roberts, Williams and Jones. It is also why we went to church and always wore suits and dresses as traditional clothing instead of boubous and warambas like our Wolof or Mandinka neighbours.

We also did not have a native African language; we had a language that was a dialect of English like Patois in Jamaica. When I discovered my family were only Christian because of the effects of the transatlantic slave trade and that the area we lived in was originally made up of African Muslims, I set out to study my history, including the Mali and Songhai[44] empires and the spread of Islam in West Africa.

I was six or seven years old when I decided to compare Christianity with Islam, and Islam made the most sense. Also, the area I came from was demographically Muslim. So I decided that when I grew up, I would be a Muslim. Before colonialisation, the African empires were Muslim. West Africans traded with Arabs and Berbers[45] from the North, discovered the religion from them and became Muslim, which was a very peaceful process compared to the colonialisation which brought Christianity to the region.

I was an avid reader from an early age. My mum refused to buy me video games, and instead, she took me to the library and encouraged me to read books. This was how I grew up with a

---

[43] Ethnic groups formed during the European colonial era from the mass displacement of peoples.

[44] Great trading state of West Africa, which controlled more gold and conducted more global trade than any European power in the fifteenth and sixteenth centuries.

[45] An ethnic group indigenous to Morocco, Algeria, Tunisia and Libya.

passion for reading, even at church while others were talking about what was happening in church, I would pick up the Bible and start reading it. I was also into history and spirituality, and reading the Bible led me to know quite a bit of Christianity for a child my age or perhaps even older. That year, when I was seven or eight, my grandma took me to the Gambia, where I kept hearing a shouting noise five times a day. I wanted to know what it was. I was told it was the Muslims and that was their call to prayer. I thought that was interesting.

Whenever I went out onto the streets, I saw pictures of a particular man everywhere: on the backs of taxis, in shop windows and in the buildings. He had big eyes, a turban and a beard. I felt I had to know who he was and why he was so important to the people there. I was told he was called Baye Niass[46] (rta)[47] Sheikhul Islam and Muslims respected him as their leader, guide and mentor. I felt a silent solidarity. As I saw people praying in the streets, I marvelled at how everyone in our country was Muslim, yet we were not. My grandma responded by saying it was a different religion with the same prophets as in the Bible, like Moses and Abraham, but they had an extra prophet named Muhammad (pbuh).

She then directed me to other family members who had Muslim friends in a bid to satisfy my curiosity. She had always encouraged me to learn, study and read. I remember on that trip she bought me a book about ancient Egypt, ancient Greece and ancient Rome as I was into history. When I wanted to know more about Islam, she took me to someone who introduced me to the Qur'an, and when I returned to England my grandma bought me my first Qur'an. I was young but was reading at an advanced level for my age.

I read a lot, not just to know about Islam and Christianity, but also about other religions, ancient religions and their belief

---

[46] Sheikh Ibrahim Niasse (rta) was a Senegalese major leader of the Tijani Sufi order in West Africa. His followers in the Senegambia region affectionately refer to him in Wolof as 'baye', or 'father'.

[47] Radiallahu ta'ala 'anhu (may Allah be pleased with him).

systems. I felt I understood Muslims and Christians, but in my class at school there were also Sikhs, Hindus and Jains, so I wanted to know what they believed too. I read everything I could, and by the time I was ten or eleven years old, I was sure I wanted to be Muslim as it made the most sense.

As a child going to church, I never really understood how God could be one and three at the same time. The concept of trinity and one God didn't make sense to me. It also didn't make sense to me how Jesus was the son of God and God at the same time, while Mary, his mum, had borne him out of wedlock. They never really answered my questions. I was just told it was all part of the creed, the faith.

At the same time I started reading the Qur'an, I also came across pamphlets offering information about Islam. I discovered that Jesus did not actually preach the trinity nor was he God.

When I was twelve years old, I travelled to the Gambia again. The previous year I had told myself that I was Muslim in my heart but would wait till I was eighteen to tell people officially, so no one could tell me what I could or couldn't do.

However, I kept seeing pictures everywhere of the same man in a flowing robe in shops and buildings, a man who I learnt was one of the most influential African Muslim scholars of the past one hundred years. So I was compelled to keep asking questions about him. What really intrigued me was the fact that 'Sheikhul Islam'[48] was written under his picture. I didn't know there was a Sheikhul Islam from Senegal or anywhere.

When I returned to England again I immersed myself in research via the internet on his biography. I came across the contact details of his grandson, Sheikh Hassan Cisse[49] (ra), who I sent an email to. He responded and gave me his phone number. I communicated with him via email and telephone calls. Then I

---

[48] Used in the classical era as an honorific title for outstanding scholars of Islamic sciences.

[49] The preeminent spokesperson of the Tariqa Tijaniyya, an accomplished scholar who died in 2008.

was put in contact with his younger brother, Sheikh Mahi Cisse, who was due to visit England that year. He said in a message, 'Go and visit my younger brother. I am praying and asking God that you become a Muslim'.

I went to see Sheikh Mahi Cisse and that was exactly what happened. I took my shahadah with him, he gave me my Muslim name and then I continued to keep in contact with the shuyukh[50] in Senegal. In this way, I went straight into Islam and Sufism from the beginning. By the age of thirteen, I had taken Sheikh Hassan Cisse (ra) as my sheikh, and he gave me the wird,[51] the same way he received it from his grandfather Sheikh Ibrahim Niasse (rta). I was trying to be a practicing Sufi with my five daily prayers, reading my wird in the mornings and evenings. I have been connected ever since.

Prophetic Tradition

'Indeed, Allah will say on the Day of Judgement, "Where are those who used to love one another for the sake of my Glory? Today, I will cover them in my shade when there is no shade except for mine."' (Sahih Muslim)

Supplication/Affirmation

I remember Allah as much as possible.

---

[50] Plural of sheikh.

[51] A specific spiritual exercise which comprises litanies and divine names to be performed daily.

11

Answering the call

*'O you who have believed, respond to Allah and to the
Messenger when he calls you to that which gives you life.
And know that Allah intervenes between a man and his
heart and that to Him you will be gathered.'
(8 al-Anfal:24)*

Every call requires a response, and promptness ensures a
fulfilment of rights. Muslims are required to pray five
times a day at specified times, when they are united in a
shared energy. A prayer performed in congregation with other
believers is twenty-seven times better than a prayer completed
alone. The whole is greater than the sum of the individual parts.
This is Inayat's story.

I was raised a Catholic though my dad became a Muslim
when I was eleven years old. I still went to a Catholic high school
where I didn't wear a hijab, but at home we were essentially
Muslim. It wasn't that my mum or I considered ourselves
practicing Muslims; we just followed what my dad did. We ate
halal meat, and when my dad fasted during the month of
Ramadan, my mum and I sometimes fasted with him. My dad
would listen to the Qur'an while he drove me to school, so I was
aware of Islam. However, none of my friends were Muslim or
even religious, and I grew out of it in my teenage years, trying to

fit in at school. I eventually found myself living a 'normal' secular life in the West.

Later, I had a partner whose mother was a Christian, though he didn't practise the faith as much as her. I often caught myself watching her, and I admired her relationship with God. She had real devotion; she made time for it and spent a lot of her time reading the Bible. I saw a real connection, and that had quite an impact on me. It influenced me to ask questions and find out more about religion and God.

My partner and I were quite serious about each other, and I thought we would one day get married. As I contemplated our future, I often reflected past the usual matters and on what happens next *after* this worldly life. I wondered what happens after getting married, after getting a nice house and a nice car and maybe children. I began searching for answers, and I looked closer to home. I witnessed the effects my dad's conversion to Islam on him. When I pondered my dad's commitment to a Higher Being, I suddenly realised I also wanted a relationship with God. I knew for a fact I didn't want to wait to get older like my dad or my partner's mother. I wanted to taste that connection now.

The day my dad became a Muslim, he did not tell me or my mum beforehand. Our whole lifestyle changed overnight. It really affected my mum because it all unfolded without her knowledge. She too was interested in Islam, but my dad had made jokes about it, so she was very surprised when he came home and announced that he was Muslim. I suppose he felt swept along by the whole experience the day it happened. He used to be a Christian minister and was talking about Islam with some Muslims. One day, they invited him to a seminar.

Towards the end of the seminar, right there and then, they encouraged him to take his shahadah since he professed to believe in one God. The rhetoric was you never know, you could die tomorrow! He capitulated and is happy being a Muslim now, but it can be argued that he only took his shahadah at that seminar because of the style of da'wah used back in those days.

When I became Muslim in 2009, I wanted it to be different. I told my parents about my shahadah, and I went to the mosque every day to learn. I was heavily influenced by the Salafi community; it was the prevailing culture, and I travelled around the country listening to talks. I did my basic learning of Arabic and the deen at the mosque, and I met lots of new people.

Although my first connection to Islam was through the Salafi community at the mosque, I remained open-minded to the prospect of widening my lens through travelling and learning more about how Islam is practised in other countries. I soon started a new job, and I became friendly with the only other Muslim in the company, who happened to follow the Sufi philosophy. I saw her using a prayer book from Yemen and through her recommendation, I decided to travel to Hadhramaut Valley that year. I studied there for a few months with scholars from the Ba'alawi tariqa. It was a beautiful experience and a perfect mix between conservative Islam and spirituality. I wanted to stay longer but was unable to. Then I planned to go to Syria, but the war broke out and spread across the Muslim world.

I ended up staying in the UK and learning from the scholars here. I did get the opportunity to visit Jordan and Pakistan through the charity I worked with; those trips had many spiritual benefits. Then one day, I was invited to a remembrance circle in northwest London, and the community there told me about Imam Sheikh Tijani Cisse. The experience pulled at my heart, and I wanted to know more about him. I managed to travel to Morocco to see him in person, and after that I settled in Senegal with his community where I spent a couple of years being immersed in the culture. I had a wonderfully fulfilling experience and eventually found my husband there.

To be honest, it was a real struggle trying to find a good husband. When I first became a Muslim, I was told that Allah would replace anything that I left for His sake with something better. I left my partner, and the lectures I attended made me think I had to leave my career in film and media too. I had a lot of expectations that everything would come easy straight away. I expected to find a great job, get married and have children almost immediately. But that didn't happen. It was my ex-partner that found a great job, got married and then had children. For a little while, I lost a bit of hope because I felt I had accepted Islam in my life and had given up my career but did not have the same success as my ex-partner. So that was hard and something I had to be patient with and accept as part of my journey.

I also expected that the initial spiritual high and connection to Allah I felt in the early days of my conversion would only increase, but I found myself struggling. I did not want to live Islam part-time – the thought of working in the secular world and then coming home to Islam did not appeal to me in the least. I wanted a holistic Islamic lifestyle that encompassed all areas of my life. I saw lots of people around me who still did not understand the Qur'an after years of being Muslim, and I wanted it to be different for me. Therefore, I put a lot of effort into learning to read and write Arabic. Though I can read and write Arabic, I am still working on understanding it fully.

I also had certain expectations of an idyllic 'Muslim community' because of what I had read in the Qur'an before becoming a Muslim. Unfortunately, the Muslim communities I have encountered seem somewhat underdeveloped in maximising well-being and survivability for all, compared to secular communities. Some Muslims can be quite individualistic and only interested in a friendship if you are popular in the community. I would even advise those embracing Islam not to look to Muslims as an example because there is no homogenous 'Muslim community'.

This is due to little social responsibility or obligation to the 'brotherhood' or 'sisterhood' amongst Muslims. To give an example, I know of many Black people who left Islam because they experienced racism from other Muslims. From a personal perspective, even when I needed help, I reached out to notable figures in the community, but the silence was deafening. The only sister who regularly checks on me is someone I met at the mosque when I first became Muslim. We stay in touch because a Muslim girl we knew committed suicide. Therefore, we always check on each other to make sure everyone is okay. When you first become a Muslim, you have a community for about two weeks, then the reality is that you are on your own unless you have your own network to fall back on. A similar thing happened to my dad – one day he had lots of Muslim friends, the next day they were gone.

Having said this, when I look back at everything that has happened since I became a Muslim, I have realised that Islam was the greatest replacement for all I gave up. The greatest gift is the fact that I am a Muslim and I have tasted the sweetness of faith. This is what my teachers meant when they said Allah would replace anything that I left for His sake with something better. They were replaced with complete contentment in my heart.

I always remember the exact moment Allah filled my heart with submission. My dad always watched programmes on the Islam Channel on Sky, and one day I decided to sit by myself and watch a talk about Islam and Christianity. When the programme ended, I got up to leave, but then the adhan came on. So just then, the idea popped into my heart to stop... sit... and listen to it. This was strange for me, because the adhan on the TV usually signalled a sort of advertisement break. However, this time I was inclined to really listen. As I gazed at the screen and read the translation along the bottom of it, the adhan rang out across the living room and I realised that it was *my* call to prayer.

Allah had pulled me to Him, and it was *my* time to pray. Allah called and I needed to answer. I did not know how to perform wudu exactly, but I recollected from my younger days how I had watched my dad wash his face and other parts of the body, so I did all that I could remember. Then I prayed to the best of my knowledge how I had seen my dad pray. Right there and then I decided to become a Muslim. I understood that Allah had called me personally, and I fulfilled His command because I realised He is ubiquitous.

Prophetic Tradition

'When the iqamah for the obligatory prayer is called, then there is no prayer except the obligatory one.' (Sahih Muslim)

Supplication/Affirmation

O Powerful One (Ya Matin), nothing happens without Your knowledge. When I turn to Allah, He turns to me.

12

Hyde Park Corner

'So do not falter or cry for peace, for you will have the upper hand and Allah is with you. And He will never let your deeds go to waste.' (47 Muhammad:35)

Actions are preceded by intentions. Whatever we achieve is first created in our minds; whatever we give out comes back to us. This is Anisa's story.

I was born and raised in London, and my parents were from the Caribbean. I was always quite religious. I went to Sunday school. Most West Indian parents sent their children to Sunday school. So every Sunday I went to church and learnt about the Bible and the stories of the prophets. However, at the age of five, I questioned the priest about Jesus when he was trying to teach us the trinity. He told us Jesus was God and we had to pray to him. I didn't believe him, and in my defiance I ran away from the church. My parents were surprised I couldn't just accept the doctrine as they had.

My journey began because I felt an aversion to the Christianity I was brought up in. I still continued to go to please my parents, but as a teenager, I decided to discover what was out there for myself. However, I wasn't looking for Islam. I assumed that Islam was a religion for only Asians and Arabs as no one had ever offered to tell me about it. I had some Pakistani friends who were

Muslim, but I had no idea what it was. I guess I assumed it was an identity you were born into.

One day, I took a friend with me to Hyde Park Corner because we wanted to talk about feminism; we were quite argumentative as teenagers. As we drifted through the various crowds, we stopped when we noticed an Englishman who had the biggest crowd there. We were interested to know what he had to say that made this so.

When we got closer, we noticed he was preaching about all the different prophets, which I thought was fair enough, but then he mentioned the Prophet Muhammad (peace be upon him), and this was the first time that I heard of him (pbuh). He continued talking about the Prophet Muhammad (pbuh), explaining that his message was the same as all the other prophets. That struck a chord with me. I was frozen on the spot, and I just listened.

He went on to assert that this man, who lived over 1,400 years ago, knew about embryology, the two seas never mixing, space and all of these facts but not only was he illiterate, there were no microscopes or telescopes during his time. For me, it was only common sense that this man must have been a prophet. I told myself he must have been because the word was the same, and he came to preach and tell us to believe in one God. This was a big eye-opener for me. He continued and told stories about Ali (may Allah be pleased with him).

I felt a strong connection to him too because it was almost like I heard and I obeyed. I wanted to just become Muslim on the spot that very day. I felt so in awe of what I had heard and also because as he was leaving, he added, 'You know if you die in this state, then you know you're going to die as a non-believer.' Hearing this, I panicked. I essentially turned to my friend who was with me and said to her, 'We've got to go to your house now, I want to become a Muslim.' Her father was Moroccan, and her mother was a white convert to Islam. She could see I was resolute, so as the crowds dispersed, we made our way back to her place.

I felt an incredible feeling as we left Hyde Park Corner; I felt ecstatic that I had found what I was looking for. When we arrived at her house, I told her family I wanted to convert, and they were overjoyed and got the witnesses. At the time, I honestly hadn't even thought about things like hijab, giving up certain things or adjusting my life to fit around five daily prayers. I just knew that in my heart I believed that there was one God and this religion had given me that. When I got home and told my parents, they were quite relaxed about it. I think my family thought that it was just another fad because my brother was always diving into different religions.

On the social scene, when I informed my friends, they thought it was a joke at first because they didn't see me practising Islam noticeably. I thought wearing a hijab simply meant covering my head, so I got a bandana and that's what I wore with all my hair hanging down. When I converted, there weren't many translated books explaining Islamic worship. In fact, there wasn't a lot of easily accessible knowledge at all. I had to do a lot of the research myself as there weren't many lectures or workshops available offering new Muslims advice. We were finding out things for ourselves and teaching ourselves. There also wasn't much of a community able to teach us, so we were taking Islamic practices step by step, just finding out for ourselves.

It was a big change for me when I got pregnant with my first daughter, and that was when I decided to start practising Islam properly. By a twist of fate, one day there was a knock at my door, and I opened it to find someone I had known from school. We all knew her as an outsider, not cool or from the popular group. But there she was poised on my doorstep wearing a full hijab! Suddenly I felt like our roles had reversed, because standing before me was what I should have been and there I was coming out as a Muslim in the types of clothes I had on. I could see Islam and the hijab had elevated her so much, and I stood there in awe, secretly coveting her poise.

She exuded such confidence and also looked pious, but I noticed she had a bit of an attitude, which I thought was quite rude. I thought to myself, 'do you know who I am?' She then interrupted my thoughts and said that I needed to start practising – what was I going to teach my baby? Her words stung but sunk in. I knew I was having a baby girl. Suddenly, it was etched in my mind the need to give my baby a good clean Islamic upbringing. She then went on to suggest I go along with her, and she took me to a family in West London.

When I arrived there, a really big strong Black brother reprimanded me and said I had to change – how would I teach my child? I wept and wept because I knew what he was saying was the truth, and then he offered to let me stay with them. From that moment, I resolved to start practising Islam. I even moved from South to West London, not just myself but other members from the community as well. There was an exodus of leaving the past behind us and starting afresh, a bit like the hijra of the Muslims from Mecca to Medina.

I went into the club and announced to everyone that they would not be seeing me again, and they threw me a farewell party, which was touching. I had a big belly, so I told everyone it was because I was going to have a baby, but the reality was that I was about to embrace Islam properly.

I gave up absolutely everything: my family, my friends and TV (EastEnders was a huge part of my life). I completely shut off from the world, which I needed at the time to seclude myself from distractions to focus my heart and understand. I definitely saw the benefits, but if I could do it all over again, I wouldn't have been so strict because it was not pleasant for my non-Muslim family.

Prophetic Tradition

'There is no good envy except in two cases: a man whom Allah has given wealth and he spends it according to its right and a man whom Allah has given wisdom, and he judges by it and teaches it.' (Sahih Bukhari)

Supplication/Affirmation

O Extender (Ya Basit), You give plenty to whomever You will. When I want to change my life, I change myself first.

13

The inner voice

'And provide for them from sources they could never imagine. And whoever puts their trust in Allah, then He [alone] is sufficient for them.' (65 at-Talaq:3)

AS much as the external aspect of worship is fundamental, internal worship is also key. It allows for spiritual growth and frees up space for what you hold important. Giving people the benefit of the doubt and forgiving without a grudge deepens your ability to trust Allah and expect good to come your way. This is Sister Faizah's story.

I was part of a very prominent singing group in my community, which was quite well-known. People on the outside thought everything was great, but on the inside, I had begun to question a lot of things. God was always a part of my life because I was always searching for meaning.

Even though I didn't come from a religious home nor did we go to church, I believed from a young age. I tried attending Sunday school a few times and decided I didn't like it. I tried a church where I saw children my age dress up in nice dresses every Sunday, but something about it all didn't sit comfortably with me, so I ended up leaving. Throughout those years, I searched for a connection with God through a medium that felt right to me. When I came across the Rastafarian[52] movement, I espoused their cause because I found it new, fresh and, more importantly, it acknowledged me and my African descent. This was something that I had read about but not seen before in practice.

From an early age, my mother made it very clear to me who I was and where I originated from, so connection was important to me. In the media, I saw that the Rastafarian movement had a connection to Africa and was being recognised everywhere as a force we needed.

I excitedly became part of the movement; however, as time went on, the movement eventually split. Some viewed Emperor Haille Selassie as a manifestation of God Himself, and that was when alarm bells went off in my head. I started to think, 'I didn't sign up for this,' but I cautiously kept my thoughts to myself because everybody around me was so happy about it. I was just a young girl amongst many older people. I didn't feel I could go against the crowd and say that I didn't believe in it, so I went along with it for years. But as the incongruence became apparent and uncomfortable to contend with, I dared myself to question certain ideologies of the movement. However, I remembered that this was my community, and we went along with our community in everything. No one would ever choose to stand alone.

Then certain events unravelled in my life, things that forced me to step back and question my 'culture', or the ideas that had been imposed on us as a group. As soon as I gave myself permission to do so, I questioned *all* my beliefs, and I clearly decided what I did and didn't believe anymore. I asked myself why I was going along with it then. Was it because they were my friends? I went to school with them? We had grown up together and we made music together? Where did I stop, and where did the others begin and where were my boundaries? I asked myself

---

[52] A religious movement of Jamaican origin holding that Emperor Haile Selaisse of Ethiopia was the messiah and Black people will eventually return to their African homeland.

these fundamental questions; I wanted to know what was really important to me.

I remember the moment everything started to become clear to me; I was at home watching a programme on television presented by Ali Missouri in the early 1980s about Africa. It was footage from Northern Nigeria with veiled men riding gracefully on horses with all the regalia and attire of royalty. I was mesmerised, completely blown away by the sheer sight; I marvelled at the beauty of it all. The message I took from the video was that God likes things that are beautiful.

Then I asked myself why we were never shown anything of the sort at school. We were shown scenes of naked people crammed aboard a ship being sent across the Atlantic Ocean to be chattel slaves. I accepted this as a horrific event that happened in our history, but from what I could see from this programme, we also had a glorious past. I wanted to know more about it.

I wondered what was so unique about this group of people that despite the slavery, colonialism and underdevelopment afflicted on the African continent, they still had a strong sense of identity. These thoughts were swimming around my head and led me to focus on my connection with God, which to me was a personal affair, no matter what others said. I felt my purpose should be to communicate with God directly. I have always felt this. It was never in question, but I struggled to understand what the group was doing. Then I had some dreams that confirmed to me that I was not on the right path in my life.

I started asking who the people I had seen on the TV programme were. I learnt that they were Muslims. This led to a string of questions: What was a Muslim? What was Islam? What do they believe? What do they do? I didn't know anything about it. Someone who was a member of the Nation of Islam had come from the US, and he gave me a copy of the Qur'an. He was sincere in what he believed, but I found some of his rhetoric flawed, primarily that white people were devils. I thought I couldn't possibly accept that. Coming from the Caribbean, we were Creoles, which meant we were a mixture of many different types of people. Growing up in a family like mine, I saw the fairest and the darkest of complexions showing unconditional love to one another, so I could never accept an idea like that.

I was also always taught to treat people individually as you find them, not lump people together in groups and believe every one of them must be like this or that, because it's not the case. I was glad that I had that kind of upbringing, so I took the Qur'an from him and put it away. I left my quest there and went back to my life.

Years passed, and I went through many traumatic experiences. I should have known better and done better because I knew I was living a lie, going along with people in silence but not believing as they did deep in my heart. Then one day, a young brother I had been to college with stopped me by the roadside and asked me to buy what he had on offer. I declined. Then about two or three months later, I met the same brother again, and this time he had a leaflet in his hand, which he gave to me. When I queried what it was about, he started telling me about Islam.

I was willing to rekindle my interest in Muslims, who he also explained were distinct from the Nation of Islam. So I agreed to go along to an event simply to listen. He informed me that a lot of brothers and sisters I knew would be there. I went home and told my mother, who candidly warned me not to play with people or their religion. If I wanted to take it seriously, I should get informed and understand its practices. I assured her I was only going to have a look, to know what they really believed. But as I attended their meetings more regularly, I felt the energy, sincerity and passion from the speaker in his delivery. He had a clear connection to God, and it touched my heart. I realised that this was not too different from what I truly believed. I was intrigued and wanted to keep attending, and the more I went, the more I felt I was getting closer to what the Truth was, which was reassuring. It was also just before the holy month of Ramadan.[53]

Suddenly, I felt an intense desire to be on the right path. I realised a connection with Allah was more important than anything else around me. With my reading, my conversations with others already in the fold of Islam and my newfound understanding, I realised the adab[54] in Islam was not far from the adab that we had as people in the old-time Caribbean. People of that generation were taught to address people when they entered a room; those standing also addressed the ones sitting. The way the elders were considered, revered and treated was warm and full of respect.

I soon noticed that there wasn't anything about Islam that felt foreign to me; it didn't feel like I was learning a new set of principles. It was all very dear to my heart, and I was a bit shocked when eventually I wanted to take my shahadah, because I had earlier reassured my mother I was only looking into the religion, nothing more.

I was embraced by everyone the day I took my shahadah, and I felt as elated as one who had come home to her people. It felt so right and comfortable and after all the joyful greetings and supplications made, I went home that evening and cried and cried. I cried because it suddenly struck me that this was the Truth. I thought I would have to give up everything around me, so I also cried because I wasn't sure I was going to be strong enough to actually do that. Asking someone to give up the people that they grew up with, the community that they came from and the culture they are accustomed to is quite a serious thing. But my fears were diminished, I was filled with hope when I remembered that this was the Truth and that everything happened for a reason and Allah really is the One that makes these things take place.

---

[53] The ninth month of the Islamic calendar, observed by Muslims worldwide as a month of fasting, prayer, reflection and community.

[54] Islamic etiquette of decency, morals and good manners.

It was no accident that I met the brother; it was no accident that I came to be in the community. So after reminiscing about all that, I cried again because I knew that my whole life had changed in a moment. I wasn't going back, and I felt a warmth, a spiritual bear hug envelop me. I was crying, but I felt comforted at the same time because I was saying goodbye to something, a lifestyle, not knowing if I was strong enough to live up to the new expectations I had for myself. I was part of another community of Caribbean Muslims and this was quite exciting because everybody was seeking knowledge together and a better version of him or herself.

I must have either been extremely naïve or extremely well supported because I was not aware of different types of people in the mosques and the experience of racism amongst Muslims, neither the perpetrators nor its victims. I assumed it was all good because I was quite sheltered at the beginning. I was around a lot of the brothers and sisters who also reverted to Islam; many were seven to ten years older than I was, so I was looked after. Besides, there was a lot to learn, which was the focus. I felt like a newborn baby, and we all learnt in the community side by side.

While I acquired the knowledge I was applying to my life, I often felt mixed emotions of nervousness and excitement. To calm myself, I reminded myself of the stories I heard from my parents and that the Islamic tradition was not foreign to us Caribbean people. It was woven into the fabric of old folk tales. My parents' generation would have been about five generations away from when slavery was imposed on them. A lot of our ancestors' culture was taken away; in particular, they were not allowed to speak their native languages.

However, times changed, and my mother's generation all understood at least three languages: Spanish, English and Patois. There were different things going on around them, which caused all of them to be required. Nevertheless, the thread of Islam still underpinned many aspects of the culture. A lot of the teachings I learnt in the first couple of years as a Muslim were things I had heard my parents say. So it wasn't alien to me; it was closer to me than the movement I was in before.

The day I realised Allah was enough was like a cool breeze that blew over me. I trusted myself that I was in the right place, and I never questioned it from the moment I took my shahadah up until now, alhamdulillah. From that day, I felt sustained by my faith. I already wore long clothes and dressed modestly since my teenage days, as we weren't into exposing ourselves in ways that were frowned upon.

In this way, I found the transition to being a visible Muslim easy, though I did tone down the colours I wore when I first came into the fold. I wanted to do everything right, so I chose not to wear my bright colours. I deliberately didn't do certain things, though I had previously always been a rule breaker – a rebel some might have said. Then I read in the Qur'an that Allah does not ask you to give up everything about yourself, so there was no need to give up things from my culture that were actually beneficial, and not against Islam, so that was a relief.

I practised what I could. I wanted to ensure my actions corresponded with what Allah asks me to do because the Qur'an is a guide for making my life better and preparing me for the hereafter, which is the most important thing.

At one point, because of my 'new' beliefs, nobody from my 'community' wanted to talk to me. People I used to know would cross the road when they saw me coming. I remember once I was talking to somebody in a telephone box when someone who I used to look up to flung the door open and hurled abuse at me, shouting 'What is the matter with you? What happened to you? Look at the way you're dressed! You used to be such a nice dresser!' She made quite a scene on the main road. Throughout it all, I firmly told myself I would not respond to her. I didn't say a word, and, eventually, she got tired and walked away.

From one perspective, I was grateful to be on my own at that point because it gave me room to change and grow. I developed in confidence and became more comfortable to wear my abaya[55] and long clothes and be who I wanted to be. Allah gave me many opportunities when I was ostracised from the community that I grew up in. There are always disguised opportunities in hardship.

In one sense, I felt hurt when I realised those I had known before in my previous identity as a singer were angry with me. I made an identity switch, and they felt I had let them down by leaving their community to join a foreign religion. In the early days, they were too angry to listen, but Allah opens hearts. Now, we have civil conversations, and I am able to tell them about Islam. Even though they ostracised me, it didn't shake my faith. This reminds me of when the Quraish[56] signed the declaration to boycott all dealings with the Muslims, yet it did not deter their belief in Allah and His Messenger (pbuh).

Prophetic Tradition

'Do not be people without minds of your own, saying that if others treat you well you will treat them well and that if they do wrong you will do wrong. But instead accustom yourselves to do good if people are good and not to do wrong if they do evil.' (Tirmidhi)

Supplication/Affirmation

O All-Seeing One (Ya Baseer), I forgive myself and others. Tests are a normal part of life. I am patient when they come.

---

[55] A simple loose overgarment worn by some women in parts of the Muslim world.

[56] A grouping of Arab clans that inhabited and controlled the city of Mecca.

14

Black Jesus at the Ethiopian church

'It was thanks to Allah's Mercy that you were gentle with
them. Had you been rough, hard-hearted, they would
surely have broken away from you.' (3 Ali Imran:159)

Many who embrace Islam are looking for something to atone for their previous vices. Sincere repentance and the belief that your striving for forgiveness has been accepted is necessary to allow you to move on with confidence, guilt-free. It also removes mental blocks and fosters a relationship with the Creator centred on love and acceptance, as opposed to fear and suffering. Allah's Mercy transcends His wrath. This is Rashidah's story.

It was the year 2002. I was a proud and out Ethiopian Orthodox Christian. I fasted for Lent during Easter and was brought up going to the community church. St Augustus was for Easter and Christmas was on 7 January, the Coptic Christmas, on which were very long services requiring us to stand for hours. I always hated that part, but I generally enjoyed making friends and eating the 'body and blood' of Christ during communion.

I had many Muslim friends at secondary school and had learnt about Ramadan from a young age. It was foreign to me, but I understood what they were doing. We often compared whose fast was hardest, as our fasting seasons coincided for a few years. My brother would often come home saying 'wallahi'[57] which was a phrase he picked up from playing on the pitch with the Somali kids. I distinctly remember telling him off for saying that in our house because we were Christians, not in a Islamophobic way, but from the point of view of loyalty. We were not allowed to eat halal meat at home as a way of securing our identity.

I went into sixth form, and there I had a boyfriend who was studying Islam and Philosophy because it was the only course he could do along with History and Government and Politics. Meanwhile, I studied Biology, Chemistry and Economics. As the months went on, he would make comments like 'Islam is the truth, you know.' I said something along the lines of 'Yes, but Christianity is my truth.'

Several months went by, and he and his mates became more immersed in Islamic discussions. He shared with me their views and what they discussed. But by this point, I was in my first year of university and at the height of my party days and absolute youthful fun. The last thing I wanted to discuss was religion. Our paths began to split as I pursued life as a full-time student, Argos cashier and party girl, while he became more withdrawn from my scene. 'What's going on?' I asked. He told me he'd like me to read a booklet called *An Illustrated Guide to Islam*. He gave me the copy that I still have to this day. I was already bored. I told him I'd be open to it, but I loved my religion. We were no longer as close as we used to be because our lives had become very different. But we cared for each other, and the distance was hard. So, reluctantly, after a few days, I read it in one sitting. And I was blown away!

Then I felt confused, annoyed and betrayed. I knew I could not unlearn what I had read, so I spoke to him. He was able to answer my questions both about Islam and Christianity. I was angry for a few weeks and didn't do anything. By this point, he converted to Islam and was living a full-time new identity. He

---

[57] 'I swear to Allah,' a promise that something is true – common in London slang.

was praying and fasting away from the family home, and I was annoyed at how quickly things were changing and how difficult he was.

So I made an appointment to see Sheikh Abdul Raheem Green[58] at Regent's Park Mosque for a discussion to clear my head. I did not really know where I was headed at that moment, but people were kind, so I was open and after a few questions to begin with, I didn't really know what to ask. I was really confused and frustrated. I also felt scared at the same time because I couldn't simply switch off what I knew. I felt I had to do something about it.

I sat there realising I wanted more answers, so I asked some questions that were very basic and simple at this point. For instance, I had for some time started to wonder about the cross that I proudly wore around my neck. The sign of the cross was brought up, which we did before we ate. It was a huge symbolic sign of our adherence to our religion, and my mum expected us to abide by it. We had it all around the house; we were constantly doing the sign on our bodies. I suddenly wondered why we would use a sign of death as a sacred action; it was a thought that just came to me. It wasn't a view expressed by anyone, but I just realised that the symbol held so much suffering.

However, the hardest aspect for me was my confusion and anger about Jesus not actually dying on the cross. A lot of my frustration and anger came from that, and I felt so betrayed. I felt this couldn't be the truth, but I realised I had only read one book. Could I give up my whole identity based on the writer's claim? So I asked him a lot of questions about that. He was very patient and articulate. He explained to me with whatever little capacity I could understand because I hadn't studied this in Christianity. He was able to explain things in very simple terms, and I left there thinking he had answered my questions in a scientific way.

---

[58] A British convert to Islam who is known in Muslim communities for his da'wah work.

I felt I was on a rollercoaster of emotions because my identity was hugely wrapped up in my religion, and I pondered what I was going to do. Not coming up with any practical solutions, I decided to park it for a while, as I didn't want to put too much pressure on myself. However, at this point, things started to rapidly change in my world and lifestyle. I became disillusioned with the partying scene. I felt marred and wondered what I should do because Islam was a big dilemma for me. I felt quite scared by what I had read and by the idea that I could die at any moment. I didn't want to die in that state, and that was my biggest concern.

I didn't think I could speak to my family about this at all, but, eventually, I approached my mum and cautiously asked what she thought about Islam; she said she didn't have any thoughts on it. That conversation ended before it really started, and I knew not to push it, so I went back to my halls of residence. When I moved out of my parents' home to live in the university halls, I had found a Bible in the wardrobe on a little shelf, the King James version. For the first few weeks, I read a couple of pages a night; it was great to read the Bible in a language that was accessible to me, the stories of Judas and the story of the crucifixion became major stories for me.

My parents were very happy the day I told them I had been reading the Bible. Then I told my mother that in reading the Bible, there were a few things I hadn't understood. I also brought up a few similarities I had noticed between Christianity and Islam, such as the virgin Mary. I explained that Muslims also believed in the virgin birth. She was as surprised as I was because we didn't know any of this before.

I had always thought Islam was completely different to Christianity, but the stories in the Qur'an were familiar, so I just relaxed and told my family I was interested in it. However, there was a subtle yet clear enough message from them that spelt don't go near it. So I retreated. It was almost like a warning sign, so after I mentioned it, I left that day to return to my halls again.

I was quite confused as it was obviously something I could not afford to bring into the household. Even though we were quite tolerant of others, and as immigrants in this country we lived in communities where there were lots of different identities with lots of different religions, we were still Christians first and foremost. We were very different to the Muslims, so I was generally quite scared at what would happen if I just converted. So I needed a plan of action.

It was coming up to January, and I said to myself I would finish my exams and then take my shahadah. It was 24 January 2003, and I had made up my mind, so I said a prayer, 'Please guide me in the right path and show me the right way and make it easy for me whatever it is.' With that, I had a new sense of hope, a new sense of certainty and a feeling that it was going to be good and peaceful. And it has been ever since.

Now, as a Muslim, I still travel back to Ethiopia with my children, and we visit the churches, amongst other historical sites. We see the first land the early Muslims migrated to for safety purposes. The land where they were protected by the Ethiopian king, the Najashi. In these churches, Jesus is Black. It's important for us to witness an alternative narrative to the one propagated and widely accepted by the West.

Prophetic Tradition

'Supplicate to Allah Almighty and be certain that He will answer your prayer.' (Tirmidhi)

Supplication/Affirmation

O Perfect One in Ability (Ya Muqtadir), all power and might belong to You, and nothing is impossible for You. I seek help with prayer and patience.

15

Seeking solace

'Put your trust in Allah. Allah is sufficient a guardian.'
(33 al-Ahzab:3)

Having searched earnestly for guidance and answers, many eventually arrive at the conclusion that there is no god but God. That for them is enough, just believing in the unseen. The eye cannot unsee what it saw, the ear cannot unhear what it heard and the heart cannot unfeel what it felt. This is Aishah's story.

My husband would say I'm not a convert, or I didn't convert to Islam, and to some extent, my story is not like that of most converts, in that strictly speaking, I am a second-generation Muslim. My parents were a part of the 1960s spiritual movement, the Seekers of Truth. They both went to Oxford to study. My father studied classics and my mum, English. Separately, they both joined a new spiritual movement called Subud which was started by a Sufi Muslim called Muhammed Subuh. This was open to all, religious and non-religious, provided they believed in a Higher Power or Creator.

My father met Muslims through this group and in Oxford he met a knowledgeable convert called Ahmed Bullock who he talked a lot to and who answered many of his questions about Islam. My father's studies of the Bible in the Greek language led him to realise that the word used for 'son' in the Bible meant 'servant'. So when Jesus says that if we follow him, we can all be 'sons of God', he meant 'servants of God'.

This led my father to write extensive letters to his Christian parents, at one point even questioning the virgin birth, though he would later come to realise this was affirmed by Islam. He accepted Islam after travelling to Indonesia and Germany to Subud conferences, and my mother accepted Islam shortly afterwards as well.

This all happened before I was born, so in that sense, I was born a Muslim. My brother was born a Muslim too, as my mother was pregnant with him at the time. My sister, however, spent a year or so of her life as Laura before being given an Indonesian name meaning 'little light'. After my father finished his degree, he struggled to find a suitable post in the UK. An opportunity arose for him to travel to Nigeria to take up a position as a classics lecturer at Ibadan University, so off we all went.

My earliest memories of the journey to Nigeria were taking anti-malaria pills before getting on the plane, then eating Jollof rice in the hotel we stayed in before we got a place to live in. There were vultures on our roof, snakes and red ants near the swing in the garden. I also remember being taken out in a pram by the local kids and hurting my fingers in the pram hood and also playing in the nursery playground where I and one other boy were about the only white kids. I also remember I really loved my teacher, Mrs Ogdobesson.

Unfortunately, our time in Nigeria was cut short. It was a time of internal conflict and upheaval following independence from the colonists. One lady was murdered right outside my nursery, and her body was left for hours as locals passed without calling the police for fear of being implicated.

One night, my father's car was being mended, so he was going to walk home from the university. His friend offered him a lift, and for years I believed that he had not taken that lift, and so I carried a huge amount of anger towards him for what transpired. Forty years later, I found out that he had taken the lift and was dropped off at the end of our road. But even that was not enough, as someone was apparently lying in wait for him and stabbed him once, robbing him of his life and the tiny amount of money he was carrying.

He was discovered close to death by his work colleague, who called another colleague and then the police. So my other early memories are of my mother going to the morgue to say goodbye to him and me wanting to go with her. I have always had trouble with goodbyes ever since. I'm crying now, writing this! I also remember the funeral. I was standing with my teacher, and I saw a box go past a Land Rover. I asked her what was in the box. When she told me 'your father', I shouted, or perhaps it was a scream in my head, 'Get him out then!'

We returned to the UK soon after and stayed with my father's parents while we waited for those renting our house in Oxford to move out and also to console my grandparents after the loss of their only child. My grandparents on both sides were Christian, so we grew up learning about both Christianity and Islam. When we visited my father's mum and dad, we would attend church and Sunday school; however, my mother would remind us that we didn't worship Jesus but believed he was a prophet.

When I was a teenager, my mum remarried, and I found myself with some stepfamily who took a stricter view of Islam and were critical of the clothes I wore. One of them once told me that if I left Islam, I should be shot. Well, that was it. That and the media representation of some Muslims' response to Salman Rushdie's book convinced me it wasn't a religion I wanted to be associated with. We had moved to London by then, but I moved out to live with friends in Kent as soon as I could after my A levels.

I did not receive a grant to attend the drama schools I had gotten into, so I worked in a pizza restaurant and lived with friends in various houses while I was there. I joined Subud at the age of seventeen, and for a while, I continued to attend their gatherings from where I was. However, after I failed again to obtain a grant, I became demotivated, and the social pressures led me to experiment with some of the drugs my friends were taking. I stopped going to the gatherings and eventually wasn't even sure if I believed in God.

After a few years, I was singing at home, and a friend who I was sharing a house with asked me to be the singer in their group. We started to secure some gigs and even got ourselves a manager. He told me that I had the looks to go far and encouraged me to drop my then intentions of going to university. By then, I had become fed up and wanted to be making better use of my brain.

I had started to question the life I was living, and after some emotional upsets in my personal relationships, I started to feel depressed. I knew I didn't want to be used as a sex symbol and not use my mind, but I didn't want to leave my friend's band, ironically because I knew one of them had a tendency towards depression, and I worried that, if I left, it could have a negative effect on him.

I started university but still went to any gigs that were set up for the band. I struggled with university, having been out of education for four years. I also struggled with living on campus, even though I remained in the same city as my friends. It felt very alien to me, and I became very anxious and depressed, eventually ending up in the university sick bay. When the term ended, my state of mind was a little better, but I was still in a state of deep confusion and depression. I was forced to give up my room at the university, and with nowhere else to go, I ended up back in London at my mum's home.

My attitude towards Islam at this point was that it was a choice my parents had made. It was not my religion. After my experiences with my stepfamily, I felt that it was perhaps not my culture, and to some extent was exploring what, if anything, my culture was. Unfortunately, what I discovered about British culture was that it largely revolved around getting drunk most weekends to relieve the boredom of working life.

During my time in Kent, there were several occasions where I found myself realising the validity of Islamic ideas or even quoting the Prophet Muhammad ﷺ. When one colleague was particularly angry about something, I told him that the strongest person is the one who can restrain their anger, not the one who acts on it.

On another occasion, I was selling my first car and driving it out to a lady who had expressed interest in it. While driving, I re-experienced a disturbing mental state that I had had for a while after I had been ill as a child. At that time my mother had told me to say 'Allahu akbar' (God is greater) to make it go away. I remembered that it had usually worked and found myself saying it over and over as I drove. I quickly felt fine and went on to sell the car. Reflecting briefly on this, I felt a bit hypocritical saying 'Allahu akbar' when I didn't consider myself a Muslim, but I soon put it to the back of my mind.

By this time, my brother and sister had both accepted Islam for themselves. I understood my sister's conversion because I knew she wanted to please my mum. On the other hand, my brother's conversion shocked me. He had always been very scientific, so it puzzled me that he was convinced that Islam was true.

While in the sick bay, he gave me a book regarding the scientific miracles of the Qur'an written by an American convert. It described verses in the Qur'an I knew nothing about, in which natural phenomena such as the growth of the embryo were described with great accuracy. It also cited the nonsensical arguments people would come up with to refute such verses. One such argument was 'They probably chopped something in half to see that!,' even though some of the detail described can only be seen using a high-powered microscope that was only developed in recent years, and certainly not 1,400 years ago.

In my confusion, I posed a question to a counsellor who came to talk to me at the sick bay and was given the exact nonsensical responses cited in the book. Once back in London, I was surrounded by books and videos about Islam, which I avoided for a while, but gradually I started to look at some of them. In one video, the ludicrous nature of not believing in a Creator who created all this amazing world was argued very eloquently and convincingly. I had an English translation of the Quran. Sometimes I read it and was surprised at how many of the biblical prophets' stories were told in it. I had known Muslims believed in them, but I did not realise the Qur'an narrated their stories.

One day, still hoping to find a way to avoid becoming a Muslim, I opened the Qur'an randomly, wanting to find a verse I could disagree with. The Qur'an opened on a verse describing those who try to find fault in the Quran and fail to do so. Suddenly, I felt that something was seeing into my heart and responding directly to me.

I started to sit behind my family when they prayed and began to pray for strength to cope with the internal battle going on inside me. It seemed that the closer I came to accepting Islam, the stronger the negative force or angry voice inside me would get. One day it suddenly dawned on me. This angry force hated Islam and didn't want me to accept it. This angry force wanted me to destroy myself; it didn't want good for me.

I realised just then that Islam was good for me and must be real and that this very real negative force was not really me but was called shaytan: the rejected one who has vowed to take humans away from God by every devious means he can. That was the moment I knew without a doubt that Islam was the truth. Soon after I started to learn, or rather relearn, how to do my prayers and began to pray.

Prophetic Tradition

'No fatigue, illness, worry, sorrow, harm, grief or even the prick of a thorn afflicts a Muslim except that Allah expiates some of his sins by it.' (Sahih Bukhari)

Supplication/Affirmation

O Concealer of sins (Ya Sitteer), conceal my faults and calm my fears. Tests are a normal part of life; it will pass.

16

Following the heart

'Only those who come to Allah with a pure heart [will attain success].' (26 ash-Shuara:89)

WE use our minds to follow the current trends or even the traditions of the past, but when looking for the truth there comes a point when you choose to follow your heart. This is Ishmael's story.

Muhammad Ali, Malcolm X and Henry, my elder brother, who had been looking into Islam a few years before me, were the first people who made me look at Islam. I was nineteen years old at the time, and there were also certain hip-hop references to Allah and the Holy Qur'an that grabbed my attention. My favourite DJ on Sunday morning also used to quote references from Islamic sources. All these elements ultimately led me to my mentor Muhammad Khaja, who I met at Hyde Park Corner. He was a major inspiration as he helped me see Islam as a way of life.

I knew I had to search for the truth myself because while growing up, what I was taught in terms of religion never made 100 percent sense to me. My quest for the truth was influenced by the likes of Public Enemy,[59] Marcus Garvey,[60] Duse Muhammad Ali,[61] Muhammad Ali and Malcolm X.

During the process of learning to practise Islam, I had no expectations of myself, as I was advised to take one step at a time. I also had great people around me, including a great mentor and this made the whole transition to Islam easier.

Although at first I did feel some pressure to do certain things, I was advised by people from my background to take it at my pace, and so that stuck with me, and I followed my heart and common sense to remain grounded. The one thing I wish I would have avoided was overpreaching to my friends and family in my enthusiasm.

I must also add that Rakin, who converted/reverted to Islam one year before me, is also eighteen months older than me and was an unofficial mentor without knowing. Through another good friend, Abdul Ahad, I met Sheikh Babikir Ahmed, who taught me more about prophetic emotional intelligence, tact, diplomacy, inclusion, tolerance and love for all. I am not the finished article; I am still working on it. This teaching showed me that my actions speak louder than my words.

I also have Ustadh Qassim to thank; he warned me what to avoid: famed egomaniac teachers, so-called teachers who taught hate of other paths and fake sheikhs with outlandish claims and hidden agendas. At first, I thought he was exaggerating, but over the years many of the warnings were helpful. Ustadh Qassim also emphasised keeping it real and not being fake, which I found invigorating because this teaching allowed me to be more straightforward, a principle that makes life simpler.

---

[59] An early hip-hop group formed in New York in 1985 with political messages on American racism.

[60] A Jamaican political activist whose goal was to create a separate economy and society run for and by African Americans. He espoused that all Black people should return to Africa, which should be free of white colonial rule.

[61] Sudanese-Egyptian political activist.

Finally, I have to state that being around successfully married men like Rakin, Abdul Karim Talib Lewis and Bilal Ahmed (who were married over five years before me) gave me significant practical teachings on marriage, just through their actions. I truly believe that men looking for marriage must seek stewardship with married men in long-term stable marriages because actions speak louder than words.

Prophetic Tradition

'Do not belittle any good deed, even meeting your Muslim brother/sister with a cheerful face.' (Muslim)

Supplication/Affirmation

O Finder (Ya Wajid), You found Your beloved (s) lost and guided him. Direct my affairs and take me beyond where I think I need to be. I am always thankful.

17

Knowledge is power

'The believers are those whom when God is mentioned,
their hearts tremble and when His verses are recited to
them their faith grows and upon their Lord they rely.'
(8 al-Anfal:2)

For the most part, unlearning what has been taught in mainstream education provides the space to relearn what is meaningful from an alternative perspective. Embracing vulnerability and admitting you don't know leads to remarkable strength. This is Ruqayyah's story.

From my own perspective, I always believed in one God, so I thought that was enough. I didn't feel there was any void that needed to be filled by religion, nor did I feel I lacked in anything. I certainly wasn't looking for Islam, and I didn't know anything about it other than what I saw on television, so I never thought about it.

A friend was looking at the Nation of Islam for a little while, and that intrigued me. But when I read about it, its doctrine didn't resonate with me, and I quickly abandoned it. Some years later, my partner's friend embraced Islam. At the time, my partner was also looking for answers to questions he had. He started going to the mosque, then he brought me back literature on women in Islam. We watched some video cassettes, but again it really didn't resonate. I just thought, 'I am not interested in Islam.'

However, with my partner's encouragement, I started looking at Islam again properly. He had looked into Judaism as well as Islam, and because we were Christians, he obviously knew what Christianity told him. From his point of view, Christians were not to question anything, and the beauty he saw in Islam was that you question everything, because ultimately you must account for the way you lived your life.

He felt he would be unable to respond if all he did was follow what someone else told him. He needed to comprehend, and that was why he was looking. He thought that for any religion to be from the Creator, that religion should be perfect – the truth with no flaws in it. Also, creation ought to be able to question things. What he discovered was when you question, you will eventually arrive at the truth. This was why he really believed Islam was the truth and the right way to go. He had been looking into it a great deal before I ever did. When he was convinced, he started to share literature on aspects of it with me.

I had a strong aversion to Islam at first because of the portrayal of women in Islam in the news. I knew of people who had become Muslim, and I saw the positive impact it had had on their lives. However, I couldn't get the media's negative depiction of Muslim women as voiceless and lacking basic human rights out of my mind.

Then my partner and I visited Tunisia, 'an Islamic country'. I wasn't looking at it from an Islamic perspective, but at the hotel I got speaking to one of the porters, and he was so friendly, helpful and sincere. I got to learn that he was like this because of his religion. I was quite taken aback that someone's religion could affect their manners. I found that beautiful, but it still didn't make me want to become a Muslim.

I actually became interested in Islam when Allah put something in my heart; I'll call it faith. I had a lot of literature around the flat, and one day I picked up a book called *A Brief Guide to Understanding Islam*. I curled up, relaxed and started reading it. I ended up taking it to work with me too. I was working in the city at the time, and I continued to read the book even on my break. I remember getting quite irritated with the book at the beginning because it mentioned Prophet Muhammad ﷺ a lot, and I thought, 'Just get on with the information.' But the more I read, the more I began to understand and soften to who the Prophet ﷺ was. I soon understood why they were sending prayers on him and through that, I started to gain insight into the religion and why Muslims do certain things. It became understandable why Muslim women eschew clingy clothes and the whole dynamics and setup of things in the religion cleared for me.

There was something that prevented me from accepting Islam initially – the five daily prayers. I honestly thought they would be too difficult. I was struggling with one prayer each night before I went to bed. I was baffled how I would be able to pray five in a day! The book shattered that mental block as it showed me the logic behind it, and this was what pulled me to Islam, the logic more than anything else.

It wasn't about any character; it was just the purity of everything. I relinquished the desire to control my future. I let go of the resistance. I surrendered. Slowly, I internalised the Islamic practices and adopted some of its laws in my life. I stopped going out to drink alcohol; I understood why things were the way they were. And as a human being, a woman, I wanted people to value me for what was in my brain and not for how I looked. With regards to intoxicants, obviously they would blur my vision and perception, and I understood all of that.

I agreed and understood many of the books I read, including 'Why Was the Stone Moved?' This was written from a Christian's perspective, and thus allowed me to question my position in the grand scheme of things. A cousin of mine was also doing a lot of research on Islam at the same time, but I think it was just a step too far for her, and she turned away from it. But I carried on desiring to know more. I frequently listened to Ahmad Deedat, whose eloquence and clarity had a very profound effect on me. I admired the way he broke down concepts and the fact that he knew the contents of the Bible in great depth. I felt he really understood my thought processes as a Christian.

Eventually, I had nowhere to hide; I had to admit that I believed that Islam was the right religion. I believed in all the prophets I had learnt about as a child; they were all within Islam. But the only prophet I had not known about was Muhammad ﷺ. Here was where Christianity stopped. I compared that to the way that Jews rejected Jesus but Christians accepted him. Now even though they know it to be true, they both rejected the Prophet Muhammad ﷺ.

I consider Islam as the final religion, the final phase in Allah's guidance to humankind, so I felt it became the inevitable step to take if I wanted salvation. When I realised it was similar to Christianity, it wasn't too difficult to accept, though there were major things I had to accept about Jesus. For instance, I had to renounce that he was God or divine. I always believed there was one God. I never really thought Jesus was God, so I accepted he was a prophet. It all came from a gradual thought process; I knew that if I had wanted salvation as a Christian, I had not been a fantastic one. Now, I wanted to please Allah. But I never thought that I would actually take my shahadah.

My partner and I were *both* gravitating towards Islam now, but we had not disclosed to each other we were considering taking the shahadah. I think we saw our paths to Allah were individual. However, we planned on getting married, so we approached a sheikh who informed us that he couldn't marry us unless we were Muslim. He gave us our options moving forward and left us to consider them. We ended up taking our shahadah on the same day and decided to wait before getting married.

After my shahadah, I went home, had a ghusl[62] and then called my mum to surprise her by telling her I was a Muslim, but she surprised me saying she already knew. I asked, 'How could

---

[62] Full body ritual wash after sexual intercourse, ejaculation, menstrual cycle and accepting Islam.

you know? I haven't told anyone.' She said it was inevitable; she had been observing me over a period of time, reading me and saw the transformation I went through. My dress sense changed, and there was more. She thought it was only a matter of time before I went down that road. That was just the beginning of another journey.

Four months to the day we both took our shahadah, my partner and I got married. Once in the deen, I learnt how to pray and how to carry out other rituals. I was zealous and excited; I wanted to change everything about myself and become an ideal Muslim. Then I realised that was never going to happen because Muslims, like everyone else, have daily struggles, which are always going to come along because Allah states 'Don't say "I believe" and think that life is going to be easy.' It won't be a walk in the park; it's actually where the struggle begins in its own different way. Saying the shahadah is the beginning, the easy part, but it's not going to stay easy. It just means an acceptance that Allah is One and that Prophet Muhammad, His peace be upon him, is the last of the prophets.

As new Muslims, my husband and I took things at our own pace because of the way we found Islam. Although he had been looking into it for a while, my route into Islam was basically on my terms, so I wasn't forced to do anything. I did have people around me telling and showing me what to do, and I was very keen to be visible as a Muslim and put on the veil. I was also keen to learn and apply what I knew as I felt knowledge was power. It offers more choices and the freedom to implement what you know.

I craved knowledge, and I wouldn't say it was plain sailing acquiring it. The one thing I would have liked more is if my acceptance of Islam had come to me earlier so that I could have started learning even sooner. When I had my children, I put learning off for a while. It was not necessary to do that because women and their children are present learning their religion in learning environments today. When I got married and entered motherhood, I didn't have an environment around me that encouraged studying the religion and looking after children at the same time. I did seek it but perhaps in the wrong places. Allah is the best of planners, and nothing happens before its time. When I did become a student of knowledge, that was the time that Allah had written for me, and I have not looked back since.

Prophetic Tradition

'Whoever travels a path in search of knowledge, Allah makes easy for him a path to Paradise.' (Sahih Muslim)

Supplication/Affirmation

O Provider (Ya Razzaq), I believe I can do anything.

18

When the seeker is ready

'Never can anything befall us except what God has decreed! He is our Lord Supreme; in God let the believers put their trust.' (9 at-Taubah:51)

Being open-minded is a necessary trait to learn anything. When we are fixed in what we think we know or can know, it limits growth and development. Believing anything is possible leads to just that. This is Umm Muhammad's story.

I travelled extensively while growing up, and I visited the Middle East on numerous occasions. I enjoyed the culture, the food, the music and especially the old black and white Egyptian movies starring Abdul Halim Hafez[63] and Farid al-Atrash.[64] I had many Arab friends and my closest friend was an Egyptian girl called Mona; we shared my flat in London. From my travels, I met my husband in Paris; he was Syrian and we were introduced by a mutual acquaintance while I was visiting Mona. Following my marriage, I moved to Kuwait, where I was eventually to embrace Islam.

Neither my husband nor my Arab friends were observant of the Islamic faith at the time, but I had an open mind when Qur'anic teachings or hadiths were told to me to make a point in

---

[63] One of the greatest Egyptian musicians, along with Umm Kulthum.
[64] Syrian Egyptian composer, singer and actor who died in 1974.

conversations. I was always interested to hear the meanings and explanations.

As a child, I often pondered the meaning of life and the existence of God. I had always believed in a Higher Power, a One, All-Powerful God figure. I came from a Christian background, and in my early years, my mother took us to church. As time passed, she remained a believer but had her own spiritual outlook. You might say I was a seeker, seeking my spiritual belief and fulfilment. On my journey, I looked into Taoism,[65] Buddhism,[66] Raj Yoga[67] and, finally, I returned to the church and got confirmed just prior to meeting my husband.

During my first five years in Kuwait, I attended an Anglican church[68] and sang in the choir. No one attempted to give me da'wah nor did anyone offer me an English translation of the Qur'an to read. I expect that in their eyes, I was of the ahl al-kitab[69] (people of the book), and so they left me to it. However, I did like to hear the occasional phrases and wisdom from the Qur'an my husband would sometimes come out with.

I worked part-time at a nursery school in Kuwait City and met other English and American teachers married to Arabs. We were a young bunch, and none of us had any children at the time. But they were all clear that their husbands had said that when they did have children, they would be brought up as practising Muslims.

After some time, I was invited to a weekly halaqah or study circle by two friends. It was held at a female professor's home, a

---

[65] Connected with philosopher Lao Tzu, who holds that humans and animals should live in balance with the universe and that the spirit of the body joins the universe after death.

[66] A belief that meditation, spiritual and physical exercises and good behaviour are ways to achieve enlightenment.

[67] A study of the human mind and the practice of transcending the body-mind-intellect complex through meditation.

[68] Following the Reformation, it developed the practices of the Church of England.

[69] Christians and Jews.

graduate from Al Azhar University.[70] I enjoyed the lessons in the circle and meeting the other students, who were all reverts married to Arab men. I explained that I was Christian and wasn't thinking of converting but was happy to learn about Islam. Within three weeks of attending, I was really looking forward to the weekly circle and had started asking many questions to the women there. Once, I asked a question regarding Prophet Isa[71] (as) to one of them, but she didn't know the answer. She said to leave it with her, and she would look it up and tell me the answer the following week. This response really perplexed me, as I had no idea what she meant or where she would look up the answer to this question I had just asked.

The following week, I eagerly awaited attending the circle and proving that this question couldn't be answered, that Islam didn't have all the answers and that I was still seeking the Truth. How wrong I was! Not only did the sister answer the question, it made perfect sense to me, and I realised there and then that this knowledge had been in my heart all along. Furthermore, these explanations of Islam resonated with the core of my very being, and I grasped that I had found the path I was looking for. Just then I realised that in all my travels, with all my Arab friends, at the circle at the house that the teacher had opened with hospitality and non-judgement, I had witnessed true Islam.

I asked the sister, where did you find that knowledge? She answered very candidly, in Fiqh al-Sunnah,[72] in the hadiths of the Prophet Muhammad ﷺ. I was so amazed; I did not know up until that time that there were books of hadiths that explained the Islamic faith's positions on how to act, to do business and to be righteous and fair in all dealings. I was blown away. I knew this to be the Absolute Truth and asked to take my shahadah.

---

[70] The most prestigious university for Islamic learning and Egypt's oldest degree-granting university.

[71] Jesus.

[72] An encyclopaedia that explains the basic practices of Islam such as salah, sawm, zakat and hajj.

A special occasion was arranged for me with gifts and good wishes. I never thought for a moment I would attend that circle and end up becoming a Muslim, alhamdullilah. There I was, a devout Christian but believing in One Almighty God, and, through His Plan and Wisdom, I became a true believer. All praises are to Allah.

Prophetic Tradition

'If Allah intends goodness for someone, He gives him understanding of the religion.' (Sahih Bukhari)

Supplication/Affirmation

O Bestower (Ya Mannan), I ask you as all praise is yours. What is meant for me will never miss me.

19

Truth in simplicity

*'So put your trust in Allah, for you are surely upon the
path of clear truth.' (27 an-Naml:79)*

L ess is more. Staying in your lane and working on yourself
without focusing too much on what you think you are or
think you should be achieving allows you to let go and let
God. This is Aziza's story.

While at college, I made a lovely friend. She was a Pakistani
lady who often invited me to hang out with her at her family's
house. Through those interactions with her family, I started to
become interested in Islam. In particular, I admired their eating
and drinking etiquettes.

My background was Seventh-day Adventist, and at the time,
I wasn't going to church. I was sixteen or seventeen years old,
and my interest in Islam came purely from being around her
family. I once asked her for a book about the religion, and she
gave me one that covered the basic tenets of Islam. It wasn't until
I read the book that I realised how similar Islam was to
Christianity. I was intrigued. Though I never intended to adopt
Islam in its entirety, my interest grew because I wanted to gain
some morals and good habits. After a while, however, I could
not deny the Truth in front of me.

Another Muslim friend spoke to me about Islam, and I learnt a lot from him and being around his family, who gave me guidance. At this point, I experimented with wearing the hijab. I wore it to various events and took it off when I got home. It was like doing a test run to see how I took to it, because at the time, I had been dressing as I wanted, like most of my friends around me. I was at an event at Brent town hall one day, and in the middle of it, I was convinced I wanted to take my shahadah. I saw some people going up on stage to take their shahadah, but I didn't want to do that, so I did it with my friend who I had met at college. She witnessed it, and that was when I stepped into the religion.

My mum was understanding throughout my journey towards Islam, but when I stepped in and changed certain habits, there was a bit of an adjustment period. It was one thing for me to talk about adopting a new way of life and quite another when I committed to doing it practically.

I wasn't strict when I came into Islam, but I was very particular about trying to get my practice of it right. Therefore, some of the things I changed may have seemed quite sudden to my mum, such as having a jug in the bathroom for istinja. She didn't understand what it was for, so I explained. Also us not wearing shoes around the house took some getting used to, but she took to that too after a while. The biggest change she noticed in me was in how I interacted with male relatives. This changed dramatically. All my cousins who were like my brothers, I wasn't as close to anymore. I had no mahram nor was I married at the time, so I was careful with my relationships involving men.

There was also the issue of my name change. Although I didn't insist my mum call me by the Muslim name I chose, it all took some getting used to and she was supportive. She was beginning to see a young lady who was very different to the one she had raised. I had grown up quite free at home; I did what I wanted, and then for her to suddenly see me abiding by all these rules was a big shock for her. I had always been comfortable walking around in minimal clothing, but that changed. I was now dressing in loose, baggy clothing and a hijab; I looked very different to how I used to look.

When I looked around me at the Muslim community, I felt the need to fit in, even though no one told me I had to. There were, however, discussions around what was and was not appropriate, so I tried to follow those guidelines. At some point, I felt a bit paranoid about my clothing being transparent at times, but I soon snapped out of that before it consumed me! It was almost as though some measured the strength of their spiritual fitness by their hijab, and I didn't think it needed to be that way. God looks at our hearts, not at our appearances.

When I first took my shahadah, there was no feeling of elation. It was more – am I sure about this? It was a big decision and a huge step. I thought the niqab was mandatory and I would have to grow into it in time; later, I was told it was optional. I felt at home with the Muslim community, and I was very pleased with the people I had around me though they were quite different to the friends I used to hang around with. That was a bit of a difficult transition to make, but I certainly knew why I was doing it, so it was worth the sacrifice.

I think that when there is a bigger purpose, you commit to it anyway despite the discomfort. The discomfort came from both within the Muslim community and outside of it, for instance, my expectations of people that were not fulfilled. One of the things I expected coming into Islam was that everybody was going to be accepting, but not everyone was. It was quite lonely at times, but I was very blessed that I had a strong affinity with a circle of Black British Muslims at a weekly class I attended. This was extremely helpful in my early days as it reinforced my faith and beliefs.

Seeing people of my own culture validated my place within Islam and alleviated a lot of the influence from the Asian Pakistani community over me. The level of racism amongst Muslims disappointed me; I could tell there was a glass wall. Though people greeted me warmly, it was very clear that I was not privy to certain things and I knew they would never embrace me in their family. If I wanted to get married to one of their sons, it would not happen. I could see their ignorance, which was understandable because it had been perpetuated by cultural views and biases.

Islam promotes us living together as one community, so it was quite a shock to find there was a line that could not be crossed if I wanted to truly be embraced and accepted by those from different backgrounds. My idealism was quickly put in its place by what I witnessed. I knew people who came into Islam and left because of the lack of support from the wider Muslim community. It takes many different reasons for people to come in. There were questions I had to ask myself. Was I ignoring some issues going on within me at a deeper level? I didn't have the tools or the resources then to really understand.

There was also a well-intended pressure or expectation to get married as soon as I took my shahadah. Generally, people said this was to avoid committing zina (fornication). However, going through the process of being grounded in faith and wholeheartedness takes time. Time also builds certainty in who you are and your future decisions; it really builds character. Marriage is half of the deen, but knowing yourself is the other half, so you need both. Without you, the marriage won't flourish. The narrative to get married straight away needs to be changed so that each spouse has something of value to offer the other.

Throughout my quest, things happened that reinforced my decision. After a while, I realised if I knew it was true and I did not do it, I would be denying myself simply because I thought it might be hard. Eventually I thought, 'Just do it and see what happens.' I didn't read the whole Qur'an prior to taking my shahadah. My route was a very minimalistic one. Islam is simple.

Prophetic Tradition

'Religion is very easy and whoever overburdens himself in his religion will not be able to continue that way.' (Sahih Bukhari)

Supplication/Affirmation

O Especially Merciful One (Ya Raheem), everything is working out for my highest good.

20

Lawbreakers break down
before God

*'Say, [O Prophet, that Allah says] "O My servants who
have exceeded the limits against their souls! Do not lose
hope in Allah's Mercy, for Allah certainly forgives all
sins. He is indeed the All-Forgiving, Most Merciful."'*
(39 az-Zumar:53)

W E wouldn't be human if we didn't sin in some capacity.
When we acknowledge and feel contrition for past
wrongs, we allow the pain we feel, and we heal. Showing
compassion to the self for errors made is one step towards
repenting to the Creator. This is Sulaiman's story.

I first encountered Islam when I was doing a sentence. I was
locked up with a man from Morocco. At that time, I attended
the church in the prison on Sundays, but I found I always came
back weak and tired. When I mentioned this, my cellmate
suggested I come to his service, which was called Jumu'ah.[73] I
asked if it was the same God that he worshipped or an idol, and
he said it was just God. He told me about the Qur'an and how it
was revealed. I thought it sounded interesting because I could see

---

[73] Friday congregational prayer in Islam.

we were dealing with similar prophets to those mentioned in the Bible.

I went to Jumu'ah one Friday, and I liked the way they started by laying many mats out covering the floor; it looked very beautiful. Then I watched as they did a special wash, and I thought 'Wow, that's cool.' I always knew cleanliness was next to Godliness. Then an African guy stood up and called the prayer, it sounded so beautiful, and I was in awe.

Then all of a sudden I noticed these huge, hard men walking in there who were proper hardcore, and I thought this Allah must be fair because one of the guys I was looking at had a huge scar across his face covering his left eye. I came to the conclusion that if *he* is submitting himself, not just by sitting on a chair, but physically bowing down and placing his forehead on the floor to Allah, this Allah must be someone to be worshipped!

I didn't know how to pray, so I lined up next to my cellmate, but who came in the line and stood next to me? The guy with the scar, and right in front of me was the imam who led us in prayer. I followed the movements of the imam. I went in and I bowed down. However, the second time I prostrated and then lifted my head back up, I felt a peace come over me, a serenity and also an energy that I had never experienced in the church. When I finished praying, I felt a calm vibe, and when I looked at the imam, he had his hands outstretched because after the prayer they made a supplication.

When he had finished, I don't know why but a Jamaican voice within me said, 'Test him, ask him for a prayer mat.' I asked him for his prayer mat, and with a big smile, he folded it up and handed it to me. He said, 'Brother, you're welcome!' It was a cloth one, and I still have it today. He also said he would do one more for me, and he gave me a copy of an English translation of the Qur'an by Yusuf Ali. I really felt like I had something as I wrapped it up slowly. I also knew it was something powerful. I then went back to my cell, and I started to read it. My cellmate came in and showed me parts to read that were about one God because he knew I had been brought up believing in the trinity.

It was really hot the day I was released from that sentence, and I was not ready for Islam. However, just before I left, the imam made sure of something. He asked me to come over to the window where he looked me square in the eyes and told me to repeat some words after him. It was the shahadah, and I recited in Arabic word for word after him. Then I asked what that was, and he just said 'You believe, you believe. You have belief now in one God,' and with that I left the prison.

All I had was my Qur'an in my hand and that bit of lingo, which I suppose was enough because it always resonated with me on the outside. I just completed an eighteen-month sentence on the Isle of Wight. There were three prisons on that island: Parkhurst, Albany Camp Hill, and the one I was at. I wanted to get back on the road, and having spent eighteen years in and out of prison, I went straight back to my old familiar lifestyle. I had been looking after myself since the age of fourteen, not because of poverty but because I did not want to be a burden on my mum. So I did what I had to do. That was the road I was on.

About five years later, my life began to get hectic. Twelve months earlier, I had started making a substantial amount of money, through an operation called Snow White. At that time, cocaine was the recreational drug in and around London. Crack cocaine came in from Colombia through the United States and onto other countries. Films like *Scarface* and *New Jack City* were released as a public announcement to let the people know what was coming; their streets would be flooded with cocaine.

I got involved in the scene in a big way, and I also had a huge habit, which cost me £800–£900 a day. This went on for about nine months, up until I reconnected with an old friend of mine called Darren, who had a major problem with drugs. We used to take crack cocaine together. He was in love with a very beautiful Ethiopian girl, but discovered he was using drugs. These two addictions don't go hand in hand. She refused to accept his habit and ended the relationship. He accepted it and continued doing what he was doing, but his heart was broken.

I noticed he wasn't handling the breakup well; in fact, he was suicidal. Whenever he drove, he would drive too fast and make mad turns around corners. Eventually, he broke down to me and said he just felt like being run over by a bus. That was when I sensed he was not ok, but at the time I had problems of my own to face. I had a case I had to attend to at the Crown Court, which he didn't want me to go to. In fact, he begged me not to go though he did come to the first day of the trial, as he had moved in with me. I ended up going to court, and I was given a three-year sentence. I felt strange and restless the first few nights in my cell, as if something was wrong. I was sharing a cell with two other inmates, like a dormitory. They asked if I was all right, I said I wasn't feeling too well, and I didn't know what it was.

The next day, my mum visited me, and she said Darren committed suicide. That was when things started to change for me. I went to visit the prison imam, and I explained what I was going through, and from there I started practising Islam.

During that three-year sentence, I was sent to another prison that didn't have an imam, so I became the interim imam for about three months. I didn't know much but they gave me a space to get the Jumu'ah organised, which was very empowering for me, and I had a special room in my unit. After that, the official imam came in, and things really started to pick up for the Muslim inmates. We had our Jumu'ah, but then they transferred me again because they saw me as a threat. It was around the time that Islam was in the limelight regularly with political issues around the world, so I got moved out.

I wasn't given parole, but they gave me home leave. I hadn't gotten over what happened to Darren, and the partner I had didn't want to know me if I went back into prison, so I went on the run for two years. In those two years, I caused havoc everyday doing what I used to do, and I was in between two relationships as well. One had had a crush on me since I was in my teens, and the other was from Manchester. She was a Christian, and I explained to her the grief I was going through. She ran a Christian ministry and offered to help me by looking after my spiritual affairs, and she told me everything would be all right. We became close friends and that was when I got her pregnant. I begged her not to have an abortion.

This was when my Islam kicked in exponentially. There was a lot of confusion in my head with this partner, and I still didn't really finish with her properly, and I had my other relationship, and then I still had thoughts of Darren. So with all this I tried not to get involved with my past recreational activities, but I delved in a little and then that was it for me.

I told my partner I didn't know where my soul was. I had a feeling of love inside, and I wanted to go back to Islam. Interestingly, she didn't judge me or tell me to come to her church. She told me to go to a rehabilitation centre. She went to the authorities, and I got interviewed, and they secured a place for me at a top unit in Blackpool, costing £500 a week, all funded by the government.

That was where it started. I went in there with my Qur'an, and they immediately said, 'You won't be needing this because we've got an AA step programme.' They also said, 'You will need this,' and they handed me the Bible. I protested that that was my book, and they replied 'You can have it back after a week.' I thought I was only in there to chill out from my emotions; I didn't want to go back onto drugs, and I needed a break from society.

I got my Qur'an back after a week; however, a few things started to occur at the rehabilitation centre. They said I was a bit overpowering with my questions, and then when I went into a circle meeting with all the other drug addicts, there was a moment where they all started pointing the finger at me unanimously, saying I was too aggressive. I felt pressured when they were pointing and coming at me. I had read a bit about the jinn[74] in the Qur'an and how they operate. Then they rang the bell to end the session.

---

[74] Invisible beings created from smokeless fire with the propensity for good or evil according to Islamic tradition.

I went back to my room and made wudu, and then I opened the Qur'an at random. I read the page where Moses went up against Pharaoh, and he said to the pharaoh cast your magic, and then when he did, Moses put down his staff, which swallowed up the magic. The bell then rang for me to go back up to the circle and what I saw was out of this world.

I saw them for what they really were, and I felt a heat rising inside me, but something in me said, 'Control, just keep control of yourself.' So I asked the group who wanted me here and if we could have a vote. The counsellors agreed, so that put me in control of the situation. They all decided I had to leave, and they put me in a room. It was just a little room with water on the floor and a lot of flowers. I wondered what was going on, and there was something going on because I recalled a time when they left us in a room to watch some videos on alcohol and drugs while they were upstairs chanting and moving around. There was also a woman dressed all in white, and they were doing some strange things. I don't know what, but I think they were taking some energy from us, and that was their plan. That's just my opinion. Anyway, they threw me out.

They told me there were no coaches going to London, and I would have to go to Manchester and from there get back to London. They gave me £10, and I made my way to the coach station. When the coach arrived and I got on, there was only one other person there – a white girl who wore an Afghan hat. She was kind and offered me a sandwich. I said no thank you. I saw the Afghan hat as a sign, and I decided I would find a mosque when I arrived in Manchester. Forty-five minutes into the coach ride, I looked out of the window and saw cars driven by men with long beards. They were minicab drivers. I arrived at the coach station and saw a man helping a woman with her luggage.

As I came down from the coach, I asked him if he knew where the nearest mosque was. He replied, 'Go down the road, turn right, turn left and go straight down.' As I turned the first right, he came by and picked me up in his taxi. He asked, 'How are you, brother?' I said, 'I'm fine, but they tried to destroy me in the institution I was in.' 'Don't worry, you're coming to a safe place,' he said pleasantly. I went to the main central mosque in Manchester, and just as I stepped in, it was time for the Maghrib[75] prayer.

As I placed my forehead on the floor, I bawled like I had never bawled in all my life. I wept and wept. The whole congregation came over to me asking 'Are you all right, brother?' Everything, all the years of pain, the suffering and the street life all came out of my heart. It was self-effacing. Then they said, 'Brother, you can stay with us for a while.' I replied gratefully, 'No, I need to get back to London.' I didn't know Ramadan was only a week away.

When I reached London, I thought 'Right, I'm on this.' I went to Regent's Park Mosque and an old friend asked 'Are you Muslim?' I responded 'Yes, and I am looking to take this thing on full-time.' He then quizzed me, 'Are you serious? This is not a joke. It's a serious thing, and we are here for you.' Ramadan came in, and I had just got my flat, so the brothers lived with me for about six months to make sure I was solid. But they were proper hardcore in their approach and they would say things like 'No, don't follow that, brother, they are Sufis.' I asked why. There was nothing wrong with those brothers, as I had also moved with the Tablighis in the beginning. I appreciated how they took me away from the road, and I could rest in the mosque for a while, a week or maybe two. Anyway, these brothers were hardcore, and they kept me on track.

I started to straighten myself out, and then I started getting into the incense market. I heard a voice say to me 'You've turned Muslim. What are you going to do now? How are you going to feed yourself?' I saw a friend of mine, and he was selling essential oils and candles. So I thought I could get into this business because it was pure. I would also be able to pray on time and feed myself. It was just basic stuff those days. I started running around with my table of products, then a friend gave me his stall on the

---

[75] The sunset prayer in Islam.

market, and that was how I established myself and really grounded myself in commerce. Soon I was making £700–£800 profit a week in the market.

For the next few years at my stall, I was focused on one thing – going for Hajj. I needed income from pure sources. For five years, I was in my zone, and then by the sixth year, I had enough money and I went on the holy pilgrimage. I had some amazing experiences there. I went with a jamaat,[76] but I suffered a lot from racism. Overall, it was spiritually good for me, but I was shown another side that I didn't know existed in such a place where pilgrims gathered. For example, a fire broke out in Mina, and we had to find ourselves somewhere to rest. A tent became vacant, so we let the sisters go in, when some Arabs came along and started making a fuss that the sisters should leave. A very strong sister said 'No, we're not leaving. Let us eat first, and then we will have enough strength to move on again.' But the Arabs insisted; they even got the police involved, who came over and insisted we leave.

She repeated that we weren't leaving. Then one of the police officers turned and spat in the sister's face. I rushed at them to defend the sister, then they started laying down their batons on me, and two other men from our jamaat pulled me off and it all calmed down. The sister lost bits of jewellery that day; it was also significant because it taught me not to forget why I was there.

After the incident, the sister reminded me that I didn't do my Asr prayer. After she had finished hers, she asked why I didn't perform my prayer. I told her I couldn't pray there, and she said, 'What are you talking about, have you forgotten why you are here?' I said 'Shaytan is here, and I am not having it,' and she said 'No, you're being tested.' She straightened me up.

I was in another incident at the Masjid al-Haram. It was Fajr time, and I had made my wudu. I went in and I stretched out waiting for the prayer and I saw a security officer looking at me. I wondered why he was looking at me and laughing. Then he

---

[76] A group.

stopped laughing and came over to me; I thought he was coming to tell me something. Then suddenly, he leaned forward and kicked my foot like a football.

I got up to rush him, but out of nowhere a group of men appeared, they were so tall and very dark-skinned, and they had marks on their faces and white turbans on their heads. Quickly, they assembled to shield me from the situation. Otherwise I could have lost everything; they could have locked me up and tortured me. They were from Sudan, and they touched my heart.

On my return from hajj, I felt I needed to tap into the Sudanese community. I felt a lot of love from them. I was put in contact with a Sudanese sheikh living in London, and he guided me for a while. When I picked up on my spirituality, he knew I had to move on, so he asked me why I was leaving. I told him I wanted to go at it on my own, and he said I hadn't even studied Arabic yet. He wanted me to go to Sudan to learn more. He said I had a lot of power because of what I had been through, but he wanted me to channel it in one specific direction. He said I wasn't ready to leave him yet, but I left, and I have been out there ever since, and I have grown.

There were two fundamental groups that wanted me in their ranks. There was the jihadi[77] group who wanted me in their wing because of what I had been through; it was more physically challenging. Then there was the Sufi side, which was more about cleansing the heart, being close to Allah and spirituality. A Salafi group tried to recruit me at their recruitment office; their walls were plastered with machine guns, but I inclined towards the spiritual side.

Before I went for the hajj, there was a book I got called *The African Origins of Civilisation* by Cheikh Anta Diop. In that book, I saw the African purification of the ka and the ba in Egyptian Egyptology, where the ka was symbolised as two hands up in the air and the ba was symbolised as the birth of the soul. I

---

[77] Militant Islamic movements.

was not in a position to read it at that moment, so I decided to wait till I completed my hajj and return to look at the book.

When I started studying Egyptology, a lot of brothers said I didn't need to study it, but I felt I did. The ka and the ba were there before in Egypt, and it has to do with purification. The Egyptians believed that the ka was the physical body and the soul coming together. I thought that was no different to me when I went to the Kaaba because I brought my physical body, which became a spiritual body. I raised my arms to make my duas and the Kaaba represented purity. There's nothing in there; there's no idol. It's just a symbol, and then you carry out the religious rituals.

Prophetic Tradition

'God is more joyous with the repentance of one of you than you are when you find your lost animal.' (Sahih Muslim)

Supplication/Affirmation

O Self-Sufficient One (Ya Ghani), I beg of You for guidance, taqwa, chastity and self-sufficiency.

21

Her-story

'Righteousness does not consist in turning your face towards the east or towards the west; true righteousness is believing in Allah and the Last Day, the angels, the Book and the prophets, and in giving away one's property in love of Him to one's kinsmen, the orphans, the poor, the traveller, those who ask for help and for freeing slaves.' (2 al-Baqarah:177)

The earth is 70 percent water, as is the human being, who is a microcosm of the world. We are all connected and choose to either contribute to negative energy (hate) or positive energy (love) on the earth. Our energy can combine to contribute to earthquakes or world peace. What will you choose to join forces with? This is Patricia's story.

My parents were brought up in a typical Caribbean Christian faith, which continued during the arrival of the legendary Windrush generation. As children, we were encouraged to attend our local Church of England (C of E). I joined the choir, and after a while, I became a Sunday school teacher, playing the guitar and the piano. I was involved in helping to look after the young children and read appropriate Bible passages to them. I made the most of my involvement and assisted with the church's jumble sales and Easter and Christmas events. I thought my path was set from a faith perspective, but things changed as I matured in my mid twenties and when I became a mother.

My husband, the father of our three children, was very pro-Black.[78] He came from a similar background to mine. Rather than following the path of our parents, we chose to focus our attention on African history. We educated our children on the premise that Africans and Caribbeans alike were great people. This was important because in and around London there were several protests in response to the injustices Black people were facing at the hands of the police.

We were also aware of the lies that had been spun about African history beginning with slavery, lies that couldn't be further from the truth. We all knew that African history was interrupted by slavery. We refused to accept the false narratives, and it was important to read up and follow the truths about how great African history was, as being proud of where we came from is what allowed us to elevate to where we are today.

Finding out more over the years about how Black people were treated while being taught at school that everyone had equal rights sent me mixed messages. I didn't want to be part of the establishment that propagated the status quo. Even though I had a great childhood; I was naïve and ignorant to the truth. I assumed back then that things were as they were meant to be, until I grew and matured and realised there were always options.

From there, I read to acquire a better understanding since my parents did not enlighten us on our great African history. Instead, they shared with us how things were in their time growing up, which was a real hardship.

At school, we were taught the history of the Tudors and the many other English kings and queens who reigned, but as Africans we too had our own wealth of history with *our* kings and queens. There are also other great leaders, such as Haille Selassie, emperor of Ethiopia, a country never colonised by Europe; the great Marcus Garvey, who pioneered a great shift in consciousness amongst Black people towards self-sufficiency;

---

[78] A lifestyle that encourages economic growth and development of Black people as a whole with the purpose of increasing wealth and love.

Shaka Zulu, who created a fighting force second to none that challenged the British Empire for domination of Southern Africa and Steven Biko a grassroots anti-apartheid activist.

As a result, for the last twenty years or so, I have always been in support of the cause of my people. I would do everything and anything to show my solidarity to humanity. I felt that was better than turning my back and focusing only on my family and my life. What affects my people affects me. If my people are well, then I am well. Prophet Muhammad (pbuh) spoke to this in his continual compassion for Muslims and Non-Muslims alike. I still feel uncomfortable that some people know the truth, yet do nothing whatsoever to change the dominant perspective (an example of this is reparations).[79]

With regards to my faith, I did not search for Islam; it came to me partly because of the crowd I was in. My profession as an English teacher meant I taught groups of sisters, and that was how it started. They were my students at an outreach centre. My teaching started off with ESOL[80] classes for people who had come to the UK, whether as refugees or just as newcomers to the country.

I felt there is spirituality in Islam. I believed there is a higher realm, a Higher Being, and I believed that there is One Almighty. I was happy that my people were in this faith, which was more believable to me than Christianity, Catholicism or Buddhism. I knew I didn't want to follow the Christian faith. From the books I had read, I knew that Africa had the longest history, and it is where life began. It had long influenced spirituality and togetherness.

There was no pressure at all from anyone or anything on my journey to Islam; it was amazing and so straightforward. I frequently visited my local mosque in Wembley, where I heard

---

[79] The action of making amends for a wrong one has done by providing payment or other assistance to those who have been wronged.

[80] English for speakers of other languages, classes taken by those learning English as a new resident in an English-speaking country.

sermons and sat and talked to sisters afterwards. Just before my shahadah, I shared my opinions and people asked me my reasons for wanting to convert. Once all that had been discussed, we just went ahead and I said the dual testimony of faith, which was really freeing.

I continued to visit a couple of mosques in my area. I enjoyed attending because they were full of my sisters, their children and my children. It really felt like one big family, as I do feel our faith is. I am very much a fitness fanatic and so is one of my best girlfriends, a Somali Muslim sister. We did so much together. We also accompanied each other for the Eid gatherings held at our local mosque. My family held no negative feelings towards Islam. Everybody really embraced my Islam, and I led a very freeing life. My parents were always very supportive of me breaking into my teaching career, which was where my Islamic journey began. I loved teaching the Somali sisters, for whom everything is about the Islamic faith, giving oneself to Allah, working on the heart and doing one's best for the family and community.

I love and humbly respect my sister Luna, who unfortunately was a victim of female genitalia mutilation.[81] She is such a survivor, and I am in awe of her. She left Somalia to travel via Italy to arrive in the UK. She had a child who unfortunately got involved in drugs, and she literally lost him to that, but she still survived. She's a homeowner now and works to support herself and is very faithful to Allah, especially after all her tribulations, which is so commendable. Together we support each other.

Praising Allah everyday gives me strength; it gives me light in my life, and it is a gift waking up everyday wanting to share that with my family and friends. I think one of the good things about being a teacher is you don't try to convince your students of anything. Rather you show them, and there are so many ways of doing that. There is none better than being understanding, sharing your own experiences and, in some instances, praying for them for whatever troubles they have. It gives them some hope,

---

[81] The ritual cutting or removal of some or all of the external female genitalia.

and this makes me grateful. All glory belongs to Allah; this is important.

From a career perspective, I toyed with the idea of going into teaching or law because I loved both. I had an opportunity to work within the criminal justice sector, or in a corporate setting as a paralegal for our people. Our young people are being forced into spiderwebs of premeditated institutional traps, including drug, gun and knife crimes. At the time, I felt that I could make a difference, but circumstances revolving around the events of 9/11 and the Twin Towers in America took me in another direction. This opened up an opportunity to travel; from there, I started teaching.

It has been a fabulous journey, and we are dealt the cards we are dealt. Moving forward, I have no complaints. I am blessed to wake up every day with a giving heart to whatever we face. The rest is history. My partner and I grew towards the faith together, but he didn't feel the need to convert. He calls himself the United Nations. They view themselves as Africans; they are great and therefore do not need a faith in order to prove that, so he didn't go the full way into Islam. But he is still very much a force to be reckoned with when it comes to defending the rights of Black people.

Prophetic Tradition

"'Support your brother whether he is an oppressor or oppressed." A man asked, "O Messenger of Allah, I should support him if he is oppressed, but how should I support him if he is an oppressor?" The Prophet (pbuh) said "Support him by preventing him from practising oppression."' (Sahih Bukhari)

Supplication/Affirmation

O Ever Near One (Ya Qareeb), I am safe.

22

From choir boy to imam

*'When it is recited to them, they declare, "We believe in it.
This is definitely the truth from our Lord. We had
already submitted [as Muslims] before this." Those will
be given their reward twice for what they patiently
endured and because they avert evil through good, and
from what We have provided they spend.'*
(28 al-Qasas:53–54)

IN rising above our base animalistic desires, we make use of our intellect ('aql). For many, the everyday routine of eat, sleep, work, repeat just isn't satisfying. For some, they are hungry for more from life, a deep connection that can only be attained in the Divine. This is Imam Adeyinka's story.

I did not convert to Islam; I entered Islam. That's actually how the Creator describes the journey of a person becoming Muslim in the Divine Quran. Sometimes I tell people I awakened to Islam or that I embraced it. I do not describe myself as a convert, or a revert for that matter, because one of the meanings of conversion is to be persuaded to change your religion, not just to change your religion to another. I wasn't persuaded to become Muslim by anyone; it was something that God was guiding me towards internally through certain experiences I began having from the age of twelve.

After I entered Islam, my late father informed me that we were the descendants of Muslims. This was a pleasant surprise. My great-great-grandparents on my father's side were Muslims in Brazil, and a number of people in my extended paternal family from the Nigerian side are Muslims to this day. Even though my paternal relatives are mostly Catholic, a few of them have Muslim middle names, which I found interesting.

I was born into a Christian family in America; my Yoruba father had a Catholic background. I believe there are clues that he accepted Islam before he passed away, and Allah knows best. My African American mother comes from a Baptist background, and I went to church on Sundays and to a Christian private school for my elementary school. I have early memories of going to church, Sunday school, and the main church service in Cincinnati, Ohio. Then we moved to Nigeria when I was six years old, and we did the same thing in Lagos, Nigeria, where I also attended a private Christian elementary school.

By the age of twelve or thirteen, I had been going to church and Sunday school for many years, but I was never really committed. I acted like a lot of my friends who were nominal Christians. We would try to be good and watch our language, would not steal or hurt anybody, but other than that, we weren't going any deeper into studying or living the scriptures. A lot of my life was influenced by Nigerian and American pop music and pop culture, and so, after my parents, I looked to pop icons as my role models. They were the most important figures to me. That was how it was until I was thirteen years of age, and a friend of mine became an evangelical born-again Christian.

One day, he pointed out to me that I was not really representing the faith in some of my language (which was a bit colourful!). He asked if I was Christian, why do I speak that way? That was the first time in my life that I stopped to consider if I wanted to live my life in accordance with God's will. That was when I started to take religion seriously. It was a turning point for me, and I started to read the Bible on my own quite regularly, not just when I went to Sunday school.

When I was fourteen, we moved back to the United States and we joined my mother's Baptist church. I became very active: I was in the youth club and the choir, and I attended church services and Sunday school. I was very committed and sometimes I gave short sermons at the church, but then at the age of sixteen, something started to happen. As I began learning about my history, as a young Black person, I learnt about Black history and the views of Malcolm X and I started to ask more and more questions about why the world is the way it is.

During this period, I listened to Minister Louis Farrakhan from the Nation of Islam, and I read books by Elijah Muhammad, George M. James, Anthony Browder, Dr Francis Cress Welsing, Haki Madhubuti, Bobby Seale, Ben Ammi and others. I was listening a lot to Malcolm X, Louis Farrakhan, Rev Dr Martin Luther King, Jr, and other great Black liberation leaders as well.

Some of the rap music I listened to by the Five Percenters had a lot of Arabic and Muslim phrases in it. For example, Rakim said on a track 'All praise is due to Allah and that's a blessing'; Poor Righteous Teachers used a phrase in one of their songs 'Islamically I drop it'; X-Clan would mention Adam, Moses and Jesus (peace and blessings be upon them). They would also mention Osiris and Horus and in the next breath mention Muhammad ﷺ. I heard all this from the rap music I was listening to, a lot of what they call 'conscious hip-hop'.

I was getting a lot of exposure to Islamic language, not really the concepts, just vocabulary through the music I was listening to. The more I rapped those songs, the more open I became to new ideas about how to relate to the Creator, and, ultimately, the watershed moment came when I was selected, or rather blessed, to go to on a cultural exchange programme with eleven other American students called the Mickey Leland Kibbutz Internship Programme.

We went to Israel, sponsored by an organisation internship programme, which is still in operation. It was set up by Mickey Leland, an African American Congressman, a Democrat. He started the programme because after his visits to Israel he felt that it would be advantageous and beneficial for American youth to share something of the experience that he did.

American high school students would go for six weeks and stay with Israeli and Palestinian families. They would go to historical and religious sites. They would learn about the politics and the history of the land, learn about the different religions, not just Islam, Christianity and Judaism but the Bahá'í faith [82] and other religions like the Druze. It was the first time I had been out of the country other than the seven years I had spent in Nigeria, and the trip changed my life completely!

It forced me to ask hard existential questions that I really had not asked myself since I was twelve years old. I was meeting people of different religions and visiting lots of places in Jerusalem, which is really the best place in the world to feel the presence of all of the prophets and messengers (peace and blessings on them all).

The feeling was palpable. After I went to Jerusalem, we also visited mosques, synagogues and churches, and we did the whole tourist thing. We also explored nature, snorkelling in the Red Sea. We went to the Dead Sea and creeks, and we went to Masada Mountain. The beauty of Palestine is just incredible; it is a beautiful land. Allah says He has blessed the land in Chapter 17 of the Divine Quran, Surah al-Isra, the chapter of the night journey.

Most of my time was spent in the Jewish quarter, but we spent a day in the Muslim quarter, where we went to al-Aqsa. One of the highlights was visiting the Dome of the Rock. When we went into the Dome of the Rock, I felt a serenity, a calmness and peace as I was entranced by the few people in worship, doing salah. They were just so quiet; I found their salah was so beautiful, as was the masjid. Anyone who has visited the Dome of the Rock can attest to the magnificent architecture of Sultan Sulaiman the Magnificent who did an exquisite job of making the Dome of

---

[82] They believe in the oneness of humanity and devote themselves to the abolition of racial, class and religious prejudices.

the Rock a place that reminds you of Paradise. I saw the rock that the Prophet ﷺ is believed to have made his ascension from.

When we arrived at the Dome of the Rock, there was an elderly man sitting as a caretaker. My cousin, who had also been chosen for the trip, was exiting the mosque, and he had a Malcolm X T-shirt on. This was due to the success of the *Malcolm X* movie released by Spike Lee. As a result, there was a lot of swag with the movie paraphernalia attached to it. The caretaker, who had a beautiful beard, spotted my cousin in his T-shirt and said 'Assalamu alaykum'; we had learnt the response by then: 'Wa alaykum assalam'. He then asked my cousin 'Who is that man on your shirt?' We told him it was Malcolm X, an American Muslim. Then he asked us if we were Muslim. We said 'No.' Then he asked us if we believe in one God, we said 'Yes.'

Throughout the trip, my cousin and I had been talking about our feelings about what we had seen. Once we said we believed in one God, the elderly man said, 'Then in that case, you two are my brothers,' and that melted my heart! The whole scene, an elderly white Arab man, a young Black American teenager, and he called me his brother just because I said I believed that God is one. As we walked out of Jerusalem, I turned to my cousin and said 'We must go back to the United States and let all our people know, our friends, family and those in our churches that Jesus is not God.' He agreed. He actually stayed Christian, but based on what he said that day, I think he acknowledged that God is one.

I went back and I stood before my church, a congregation of about two to three thousand people, and they asked me to share the highlights of my trip. One of the things I mentioned was that I learnt in Israel that Jesus is not God and that God is one. Jesus Christ (peace and blessings be upon him) is a human being, and I met an old man who didn't try to convince me about Islam, he didn't try to debate with me, he just accepted me. I also felt that the rivers, sea, mountains and mosques and synagogues were all so beautiful. What struck me was that in the mosques and synagogues, there were no images, no paintings of God and no paintings of the prophets.

The mosques in Jerusalem were so simple but also so beautiful, and so I really had a feeling of being in a sacred space, and I was really impressed with Muslims and the resilience of the Palestinian people. Even though I wasn't one of them, I could relate to them as an African American on many levels. At one point, we went to the main masjid at al-Aqsa, and we had just walked into the masjid to visit it when it was time for one of the prayers, so they actually told us to leave. They drove us out of the masjid. They said 'Yalla! Yalla!' So even though I was kind of heartbroken that we couldn't go into the mosque, I respected the fact that they cherished their prayers enough that they told the tourists to leave. We were short on time, so we couldn't wait for them to finish praying and then go look, and so we had to leave. Although I didn't get to see the main masjid, that experience in Israel was transformative for me.

When I came back, I started to read the Bible intensely, and while I was in Israel, I met a group of African Americans called the African Hebrews of Jerusalem who had left the United States in 1967 from Chicago. They believed that they and all African Americans are the lost tribes of Israel and that our true religion is Judaism, and African Americans need to return to their true religion. Not as the European Jews practise it, or as the African Jews practise it, but go back to the original texts and practise the commandments as they were revealed. Around four hundred of them left America.

First, they went to Liberia, remained there for about two years in the wilderness, and then they moved to Israel to a place called Dimona, where they were not received warmly. Naturally, the Israelis retorted, 'Who are you to tell us that you are the real Jews?!' They experienced a lot of persecution, but when I met them, and we visited their village, it was such a beautiful, overwhelming experience for me. That really was the straw that broke the camel's back. The camel was my upbringing, and that was what tipped the scales for me, even though they weren't Muslim.

What I saw was African Americans who were doing their best in their own way to follow their leader, who they believed was a prophet, Ben Ammi. They were following the Bible as best they could and living very healthy lives. They spoke fluent English, Arabic, Hebrew and Swahili and sang beautiful gospel songs. In addition, they built their own schools by hand and the children built their school with rocks from the mountains. They had their own clinic with their own maternity ward and midwives. They also sewed most of their own clothes and grew most of their own food.

I saw the model of liberation I had been looking for, which I had not seen from most of the people I knew from the pan-African Black nationalist movements. Their efforts were more successful than others but this was the first time I actually saw it, at least at that young age. I saw those who were walking the path of liberation in the here and now, and they weren't doing it because they were following communism or socialism or Black nationalism; they were doing it because they were following revelation, as far as they understood it.

When I returned, I started reading books written by Ben Ammi, such as *God, the Black Man and Truth* and *God and the Law of Relativity*. My plan was to become a Hebrew Israelite and I was on my way. However, two things stuck out that I just could not come to terms with or make peace with.

The first thing was they did not believe in the hereafter, and something inside me, perhaps my upbringing or just my soul, told me that there was more to this life than what we have. This was a view not uncommon to mainstream Jews; many either don't believe in the afterlife, they don't put much weight on it or it's not as important as it is to Christians and Muslims.

The second thing was the chosen people complex that I saw from the African Hebrews, who believed themselves to be African Americans, Hebrew Israelites and God's chosen people. It was quite tribal, and this was the problem I also had with so-called Orthodox Judaism, which is really Eastern European Ashkenazi Judaism. There are many ways to practise Judaism;

there are Ethiopian, Iraqi, Sephardic and Moroccan Jews to name a few. With so many kinds of ways to live the Jewish faith, what is called orthodox is generally what is known as Eastern European, which is the group who believes that they are God's chosen people. It is in their prayers, their stories and in their culture, and it just didn't sit well with me. Since God is one, we should all come to God equally.

The more I studied the Bible, the more I realised that what I was looking for could not be found in Judaism as it is known and practised by most people today, nor in Christianity. After that, I came across a friend, Rodney Warr, who I had not seen for about a year. The last time I saw him, he was on his way to become a Rastafarian; he had grown dreadlocks, wore tie-dyed clothing and smoked weed. However, there he was all cleaned up with smart clothes on, Timberland boots and a kufi (a skull cap), and I asked him what happened to him. He said he had gone to Atlanta, Georgia, which was called Black Mecca; it was a hub of African American culture, history and economic prosperity.

He said he became a Muslim, and his new name was Abdul-Jabbar. He was the last person I expected would become a Muslim because of all the discipline that being a Muslim requires. Of course, there are lots of Muslims who are not disciplined, but the Islamic way of life gives way to discipline if you want the full benefit of it. There is a discipline to the practice that brings the heart to life that enables you to live a deeply spiritual life on earth.

I found a lot of logical inconsistencies with Christian theology, but the message of Jesus Christ was very clear to me: worship one God, believe that Jesus Christ is the Messiah, follow the laws that God has revealed and do so with humility, without being self-righteous in spirit or action, without relying on external ritual alone but also internalising the spiritual dimension. That was what I was finding for the most part, but I was also realising that the Christianity of today is not always based on the teachings of Jesus Christ.

I learnt that the Christianity that I had grown up with was really the Christianity of Paul, and his Christianity was really based on worshipping Jesus; the focus was on Jesus Christ. Because he wanted to appeal to non-Jews, it was no longer important to follow the commandments, and I saw that as a contradiction. I saw what I was taught about Christianity from a young age was not the same as what I read about in the words of Jesus Christ himself, in the four synoptic gospels according to Matthew, Mark, Luke and John. I felt I had to make a choice to either follow the gospels or follow institutionalised Christianity as I came to know it.

I decided to follow the gospels; I read the gospels of Matthew, Mark, Luke and John and I read the gnostic gospels. I learnt the history of how Christianity developed. I learnt that there were early Christians who believed that Jesus was a human being, that he was not God, and that was news to me. There were Christians who believed that there was one God, one Creator only, without a son or a daughter, without sharing His divinity.

Abdul-Jabbar gradually shared information about Islam with me; he really wanted me to become a Muslim. I argued with him, and we would have debates, because at this point I was very happy to be a very woke Black Christian. I wasn't even identifying myself as Christian. I told people I believed in one God and I followed Jesus, but that I didn't have a religion. Abdul-Jabbar then told me about tawheed, the Oneness of God, wudu and salah, and I really wasn't interested in any of those things.

As I continued along my path, he was very patient with me and would walk across the city (the equivalent of a fifteen to twenty minute drive), just so he could come to teach me about Islam, or rather for me to argue with him about why he was wrong. I thank Allah for him; I don't know where he is now. I hope he is in good health and hope he is still on the straight path of the prophets and messengers (peace and blessings on them) and that of the Qur'an. He was so patient and so merciful, and he shared so much with me, a young seventeen-year-old.

He was a little older than me, maybe eighteen or nineteen years old, and he really challenged my mind, and so I started to read some Islamic studies books my parents had mistakenly bought one year while I was a student in Nigeria. The books meant for Muslim students were called IRK (Islamic Religious Knowledge), whereas I was supposed to have the BK (Bible Knowledge) list of books. We kept the books anyway in spite of our error, and four years later, I found those books in our home library, and I started reading them. They were very good, clear, thorough books from Nigeria. They delved into worship, beliefs and history. The more I read, the more I realised that this is what I already believed.

I realised that the religion I had been looking for already existed. Beforehand, I thought I was going to be lost. I thought I was going to have to make up something myself based on the Bible, but the more I read about what Muslims believed and the practice of Islam, I realised this was the religion that Jesus Christ (peace and blessings be upon him) practised.

One day, I sat in my physics class, and instead of listening to the teacher, I was reading a book on Islam, and it was at that very moment iman (faith) entered my heart. It had also happened when I was in Jerusalem, but it hadn't occurred to my heart to become Muslim then. Allah put in my heart the certainty that there was only one God; no one was telling me this. Prior to that day, my friend tried his best to get me to 'see the light'. However, I was very antagonistic. We were good friends and I had friendly debates with him, but I was not accepting Islam. It wasn't till that afternoon that I said 'Yes, this is truth, Islam is truth.' At lunchtime, I said to one of my friends, Jawad, that I was going to be Muslim, and I wanted him to give me my shahadah. However, he wasn't Muslim. Still I knew that I couldn't become Muslim until I bore witness. So I asked him to be my witness; I didn't know you had to have two witnesses.

After I said the shahadah during my high school lunch break, I told Abdul-Jabbar that I was Muslim. I told him I had said my dual testification of faith, and he asked 'To who?' When I told him, he said I would have to say it again because Jawad wasn't Muslim! So I said it again with Abdul-Jabbar over the phone, so it was official. I was Muslim; it felt incredible and amazing. He began coming to my house again to teach me, and then he told me he was a Shia Muslim and I had to choose. He said, 'Now that you've chosen Islam, you have to choose which path you're going to take in Islam' and I had no idea what he was talking about: Sunni and Shia? I thought all Muslims were the same at that point. I thought Sunni, Shia and the Nation of Islam were all denominations of Islam.

I decided I was not interested in that because none of the books I had read mentioned any of it. I was not interested in denominations; I just wanted to follow what Jesus Christ, Moses, Abraham and Prophet Muhammad ﷺ did. I then read a book that my uncle loaned me called *The World's Major Religions* by Huston Smith. As I read that book, I looked at Christianity again, and it didn't speak to my heart or my reason. I then looked at Judaism once more, and, again, it was too tribal, too ethnocentric for me. I looked at Buddhism, and there was no God, no Creator or acknowledgement of the All Knowing, the All Wise. I looked at Hinduism, and what I read didn't satisfy my spirit. After reading that book, it was only in Islam that I saw a continuation or any completion of the way of the ancient prophets, and so that book along with the books from Nigeria and *The Autobiography of Malcolm X* were key to me taking that ultimate step.

I read *The Autobiography of Malcolm X* the first time when I was about twelve years old and then again at sixteen or seventeen years of age. While reading it again, I saw him as a truth seeker, someone who was always ready to leave what he thought was true for a new understanding that was more aligned with facts and reason. His spirit really resonated with me.

I read the *Autobiography* a week before I gave my shahadah at lunch break. I got on my knees and prostrated and said 'Oh God, Jehovah, Allah, I don't know the truth, show me the path, guide me to the path I should take!' I said it with complete detachment from the outcome. I wasn't Muslim then, but I prostrated. That was how I wanted to express my powerlessness and my ignorance.

To all the different people that played a role, I ask Allah to give them, their families, their children and their descendants guidance and to forgive their ancestors. As I mentioned, I was really being groomed in my youth to be a Christian minister, a Christian preacher, but Allah had other plans for me to become a student of knowledge and then an imam serving my community, alhamdulillah.

Prophetic Tradition

'When one of you calls upon Allah, let him hope for the greatest of things. Indeed, nothing has any greatness over Allah.' (Sahih Ibn Hibban)

Supplication/Affirmation

O All-Hearing One (Ya Sami), take care of my worries and grant me ease in my affairs. Indeed, You hear all prayers.

23

In the blink of an eye

'For indeed, there is ease with hardship.'
(94 al-Inshirah:5)

When a child is born, we can't wait for them to grow up and live life. When they do, we wonder where all the time has gone. In the Qur'an, Allah swears by time: 'Indeed humankind is at loss, except those who encourage one another in goodness and those who encourage one another to be patient.' We often steal from the moment, dwelling in the past or dreaming of the future. The only way to grasp life is to live in the moment and be present in the 'now'. This is Alison's story.

I'll begin by stating what my journey to Islam was not. It was not as a result of some catastrophic or life-changing event. It was not the final point on a lengthy quest for fulfilment. It was not bowing to pressure from others. It was not the latest in a long line of fads quickly forgotten. I believe that Allah guided me to this deen and had been guiding me throughout my life, although perhaps I did not recognise it as such. I was raised in London as the child of immigrants from the Caribbean who came to

England as part of the Windrush generation.[83] For me, this meant a good family background, a strong work ethic and a vibrant community that was my comfort and respite from the hostility of the 'motherland'.

From my earliest memories, the Pentecostal church was the focal point of our community, as this was the customary style of worship in the lands of my parents. Apart from the long Sunday services, there were prayer meetings, Sunday school, Bible study, church outings and activities for young and old. Church was not optional, and even in the unlikely event that parents could not attend, the children were scrubbed, dressed, groomed and sent to church in their Sunday best. The high point of the year was the Convention, when churches from all over the country descended on one area for communal worship.

I had an awareness of Muslims, as not only did I grow up with children of Caribbean parentage but also with the offspring of other immigrant families from countries such as Nigeria, Pakistan and Morocco. However, as children, we did not really discuss matters of religion in-depth. We were forging our identities and struggling to 'make it' while fulfilling parental aspirations and struggling against the negative expectations of the 'host' nation.

As an adult, I no longer attended church; however, my upbringing did not leave me and stood me in good stead for life. (To this day, I'm sure I can still reel off the names of all the books in the New Testament). I studied, worked and travelled, all the while carrying with me the deeply instilled religious and cultural principles of my childhood – above all, a belief in the Higher Power.

My family life was good. I did well in my studies and worked for many years. I was comfortable and did not feel a burning need for anything. There was no 'lifelong search' or 'quest' for

---

[83] A generation of people who arrived in the UK from the Caribbean between 1948 and 1971. They worked mainly in the National Health Service, but by 2013, they were told they had no rights to be in the UK and were treated as illegal immigrants.

change or for another religion. My path to Islam was by way of my very upbringing and life experience. There were two factors that came into play in my late twenties and early thirties.

I was looking at life in general and considered that if a person has a 'long' life of perhaps eighty or ninety years, in the overall scheme of things, that is in fact a very short time. Life is the blink of an eye.

I have always felt as if I have been protected in some way. This may seem silly to others. At times in my life, I have faced some very difficult and frightening situations, often when alone and vulnerable. However, something has always happened, or someone has always come along to help me so that the situation has not come to the worst possible conclusion. This led me to believe that there had to be more. So I thought I would take a look.

The interesting thing is that I did not feel any compulsion to look at anything other than Islam. Some people considered Judaism or Buddhism, etc., but for me, it was always Islam. Apart from the knowledge that religions are founded on the principles of faith and good actions, I don't believe that I had particular expectations of Islam or of what I would find.

The difficulty I had was finding information about the deen, as I did not just want a pamphlet. Despite being in an area densely populated by Muslims, I found it virtually impossible to get information on women's classes and did not know who it would be appropriate to approach. I was determined and not about to give up.

So one Saturday I left home, bought a scarf in a local shop and then stood outside the door of the local Islamic centre waiting for someone to come along. When a young Muslim woman arrived, it turned out that she was going to a women's circle. I asked her how to tie the scarf and then went in with her (whether it was the done thing or not). From then on, I attended the circles regularly.

After a while, I was pretty much convinced that Islam was the path for me. I had told no one about attending Islamic classes or even that I had any interest. I had isolated myself from my friends both Muslim and non-Muslim, as I wanted any decision I made to be my own.

One of the young women from the circle was a teacher at an Islamic school and asked if I would like to go to the school with her for a visit. I jumped at this invitation to see the school and to speak to the sheikh, who kindly responded to any questions I had. As it was Friday, the pupils were assembled for the Jumu'ah prayer. They were normal, fidgety, happy schoolchildren, and it was beautiful to see how the school day was centred around the faith. I went to talk with the sheikh, whom I found to be a deeply knowledgeable, practical and kind man.

Inside, I already felt that Islam was calling out to me; however, I was very anxious and was being held back by the possible reaction of my parents and the effect on my family, with whom I was very close. I spoke with him about the possible difficulties of being a Muslim in a non-Muslim household and gave the example of halal food and not being able to guarantee that all food prepared would be halal. The sheikh wisely told me that as long as it was not pork, I should say 'bismillah' and eat the food. He added 'if your situation was different, then the advice would be different. Don't anger your mother. She is your mother.' On hearing his words, all my reluctance and every qualm melted away, and I felt as if a great weight had been lifted from me.

There and then, I decided that I was going to embrace Islam, as that was the right path for me. The sheikh reassembled the school, and I took my shahadah with all of the children repeating the words with me. Amidst many hugs and tears, I became a Muslim and began to travel a different path, encountering numerous tests and trials along the way.

The day I took my shahadah, I had not left home with the intention of taking it or with any inkling that this was what would take place that day. However, it was written for me that, on that Friday during Ramadan, I would become a Muslim. I think it is true to say that rather than me finding Islam, Islam found me after I had knocked on the door to learn what was on the other side.

Prophetic Tradition

'Hoping for good is also an act of worship of Allah.' (Tirmidhi)

Supplication/Affirmation

O the One (Ya Wahid), I seek Your protection from knowingly associating partners with You and seek Your forgiveness for unknowingly doing so.

24

An engine of love

*'If you love God, follow me, and God will love you and
forgive you your sins, for God is much-Forgiving, a
dispenser of grace.' (3 Al-Imran:31)*

WE all desire to reciprocate unconditional love. Everyone
wishes to be accepted for who they are, flaws and all
despite prejudiced views held by others. Whatever we give out,
we receive. When we love Allah and His Messenger (pbuh), we
experience the love of self and the reflection of everything
around us. When we take one step towards Allah, He takes ten
steps towards us. This is Sukina's story.

I was born into a family of people inspired by Rastafarianism.
Some of my family members had been Rastafarians but were not
anymore. But it inspired my childhood and the formation of my
spiritual ideas. Neither of my parents were Rastafarians by the
time I was born, so it wasn't imposed upon me growing up. My
aunt, who was a Rastafarian, was very influential in my life
spiritually and so was my older brother. We have different fathers,
and his father is the equivalent of a sheikh or community leader
in the Rastafarian movement. Because of this, the culture and
tradition felt like home to me.

I was raised in a Christian background like a lot of Caribbean
people, but I didn't feel any spiritual connection at school (I
went to a Church of England school and later a Roman Catholic

high school) or at church; none of it moved my soul. The Rastafarian movement was in my roots. I remember when I was sixteen years old playing an old Bob Marley cassette. It wasn't the most popular album of his, but when I heard it, it felt so familiar. I just knew I knew the music. My auntie then told me that when my mother was pregnant with me, this was the album she played all the time.

My roots gave me a solid foundation, a knowledge of self and what it meant to be a Black woman, someone from Africa and someone who was enslaved. It also showed me what resilience looked like, what it meant to oppose oppression; all this was part and parcel of my foundation, and it served me as I got older. From there I went on my own spiritual journey.

I was raised with more than one faith, so I questioned things. I had a Rastafarian background, but we operated within a Christian context, so this aroused a lot of questions in me. Not deep, existential ones like 'Who is God?' but simple questions along the lines of: 'Jesus is white, but what do we believe?' I believe this multifaith framework gave me the space I needed to question things and set out on my own journey.

Through my questioning, I discovered an organisation called the Nuwabians. It was a Black organisation from the United States that delved into different schools of thought and different spiritual faith traditions. The premise of this organisation was that Black people had been put under a spell and that religion was part of it, but to undo the spell, we had to go through the different stages of religion.

I was fifteen years old when I joined the organisation, and while there were many ideas I later disagreed with, the knowledge and information I gained later informed my journey. The one thing that they always professed was that the Prophet Muhammad ﷺ was the final messenger. When I joined, I didn't know anything about Islam nor did they promote Islam per se, but I found they never veered away from this truth. It was a truth that I accepted, so when I came to the gates of Islam, I realised I already believed that Prophet Muhammad ﷺ was the final messenger.

Later, I pursued a degree in English literature and Caribbean studies, where I chose to do a book review on the *Autobiography of Malcolm X*. Malcolm X was a figure I already had a connection with; he might as well have been my godfather. I wouldn't know my existence outside of knowing Malcolm X. Where I am from in Bristol, our local community centre is called the Malcolm X Centre. The first book my mother ever read as an adult coming into herself was his autobiography. So I knew Malcolm, I knew his story, I had watched the film and I had read his books before. But reading his autobiography at that point and in an academic way shifted my relationship with him.

On the one hand, I began to look at him deeper with even more reverence. On the other hand, my then ex-boyfriend (and the person who is now my husband) had just become a Muslim, and my intransigence to Islam was real. I remember Islam was heavy on my mind in a negative way because I wasn't really into Islam. And when I found out that my ex-boyfriend was a Muslim, I thought 'Oh my God that's it, we will never get back together again.' There was no way I was going to be a Muslim.

With a heavy heart, I read the autobiography. It introduced Islam to me through the lens of someone I loved and admired – Malcolm X. As I read it, I fell in love with his journey to hajj and the peace that was transmitted through the pages. The peace and surrender he felt was quite important to me because observing this conjunctly with his clear-cut political mindset and perspective was really moving. There was a part of my soul that yearned for that also. When one is active or vocal about oppression and injustice, a certain heaviness or a weight is attached, so I too wanted ease for my soul.

My journey to Islam was quite solitary. I was writing my dissertation in my final year of university, in a studious state, reading and also procrastinating my time away. While I was writing my thesis, I was also reading up on Islam a lot. I was trying to understand and find myself, and as I read, it awakened something within me. I remember having a dialogue with myself: 'Oh my God, I'm really falling in love with this religion.' But that was not on the agenda; it was not on my to-do list.

So the journey itself was quite inward. At the time, I was living with my friend who also became a Muslim. We were living together in a house we shared with other people who weren't really on the journey to Islam, but I shared a lot of what I was thinking about with them.

When I read about the different pillars of Islam, I couldn't deny that I believed in the same concepts. I wasn't being shown anything outside of myself, which would have been the case for me with another way of life, like the Hindu tradition. It would be clear I was adopting something that wasn't mine. Islam was indeed 'a foreign expression' to me because there's a whole cultural code that goes with it, which is foreign to the average British or even the Black British way of life. Despite its foreignness, it was familiar, as everything that Islam stands for, I stand for. I would have been a hypocrite to myself if I walked away because I knew it was the truth. I'm grateful that Allah made my disposition such that when I am confronted with truth, I can't deny it, especially when it comes to the truth of God. Even when there are uncomfortable, different and cultural structures that exist within Islam, there are things that may not work for me, but I know this is the Truth.

I couldn't deny the truth in the five pillars because I believed in one God, and I believed Prophet Muhammad ﷺ was a messenger, as taught from my Nuwabian background. I liked the concept of charity and giving sadaqa, and I obviously liked the concept of Ramadan because I had been fasting prior to entering Islam. Prayer also excited me as I loved to pray. I wasn't consistent in prayer, but I liked the idea of being consistent. And as for hajj, I was inspired in the first place by the pilgrimage of Malcolm X.

I remember while reading the *Autobiography of Malcolm X*, I wanted to know if I had any other books on Islam. Looking on my bookshelf, I came across a few little pamphlets that were handed out at the freshers fair (may Allah particularly bless the sister who gave them to me). Among them was a small book called 'Who Is Muhammad ﷺ?' I started reading through it, and I began to feel a kind of love that I can't quite explain. It was warmth from my heart, and there was no conflict in it. After reading that booklet, I went to bed and woke up the next morning feeling good.

In an in-between state before I had fully woken up, I wondered to myself 'Did I fall in love last night?' 'What happened last night that made me feel this way; did I go on a date?' I then realised that I had fallen in love with the Prophet Muhammad ﷺ, and that love has been a factor that has kept me on the path even till today. That love has been a guiding force and a motivator. Alongside the pursuit of wisdom, knowledge and truth was this engine of love. I really felt like I had fallen in love with the Prophet ﷺ that night. I felt a tenderness, a gentleness and a safety from the Prophet ﷺ: in no way was this someone who would hurt me.

Then I was put in touch with brother Ishmael from Mecca2Medina.[84] He was attending poetry nights at a scene that I was a part of, a non-Muslim arts platform of conscious Black creative artists. I had seen him a few times before. I was then introduced to Rakin, also from Mecca2Medina and his family. It was nice to see Islam from not only a Black framework but a framework of other creatives as well. I am grateful for meeting them as they were very helpful at the beginning of my journey and in understanding that I didn't have to lose myself to be a Muslim.

Mecca2Medina had organised an event at Friends House in London, and it was around this point that I decided I did want to become a Muslim. It was also the first time I ever witnessed the Qur'an being recited. It was brother Hassen Rasool, and I wept. Then a brother called Lukman from the Khayal Theatre gave a keynote talk about the role of the poets in Islam.

---

[84] Pioneering British Islamic, hiphop nasheed group founded in 1996.

He mentioned every prophet had their miracle that was connected to the people of their time. Prophet Isa (as) came with healing, by bringing someone back from the dead and curing someone of leprosy. That was significant within the context of his time. Prophet Musa (as) had a miracle that allowed him to compete with the magicians; that was significant at his time. Prophet Muhammad ﷺ was given the miracle of the Qur'an, and given the context of poets, orators and people of expression; that had deep significance for me.

As a poet and a rapper, to come to hear this explanation made me feel like I could see myself as a Muslim. My friend and I decided we wanted to take our shahadah. We travelled to Luton to take our shahadah with Brother Lukman. It was a nice community, not a community I have been back to visit, but a community of Sufis, people of faith and a gentleness that was nice to be welcomed into. I remember feeling very warmed by the experience. I didn't experience much resistance in terms of becoming a Muslim because everyone who knew me and anyone who loved me knew that I had always been on a journey.

When my close friends from my hometown found out, it wasn't a shock to them. It was just, 'sure'. Some people may have thought it was just another phase, but not my mother or my father. They understood what it meant to be of one faith and follow another tradition. I think they had been through that themselves, so there wasn't any mention of 'You can't be a Muslim; you are going against how we raised you.' My mother was more concerned I didn't lose myself, my creativity or my self-expression. My father had a lot of respect for Islam; he really respects the discipline and the seriousness of it. He also said I should make sure I know my rights as a woman.

Even in the moments where things could have been better or perhaps I could have had more support, I believe that Allah has designed me in such a way that I strive to fill voids in and around me. When I became the manager of Rumi's Cave, I realised that a lot of what I was doing there was creating the community, the space that I didn't have, a wider community. Of course, I had the early community with Mecca2Medina and the creative community, but not the wider Muslim community, a space where anyone could come to learn, to engage in knowledge and not feel like you're going to be confronted. Even if you're a musician or you don't wrap your scarf a certain way or you do not cover your head at all. A place that would never turn people away. I think that is important.

There were many who told us music is haram and I shouldn't do it. I was recently thinking how beautiful it would have been if instead of just saying no, it's haram, they said 'Let me introduce you to the beauty of tajweed,[85] of tarteel,[86] the reciters of Sudan, Kenya or West Africa.' Why not introduce someone like me to the beauty and the science in the musicality of the Qur'an? If people wanted us to stop making music, they could have given us a beautiful replacement in the Qur'an. Instead of condemning what we were doing and condemning that form of expression, they could have invited creatives like me to a form of expression in which we get to glorify and beautify our voices for Allah.

Having said that, to be honest, I don't really resonate with that stance because whatever Allah wanted is exactly what happened. I feel a lot of my work is being for others what I didn't have myself, and I wouldn't be able to be there for them if I hadn't experienced what it was like to not have that. If I didn't have any negative experiences, I wouldn't know what it felt like. I think all in all it was what it was supposed to be and I think every step of the way, every person that I met, every positive interaction and every not so positive interaction was part of the formation and the shaping of me and I am grateful for that.

---

[85] The science of phonology in reciting the Qur'an.

[86] The science defining the rules of reciting the Qur'an as taught by Jibreel (as) to Prophet Muhammad (pbuh).

Prophetic Tradition

Narrated by Abu Hurayra (ra), Allah's Messenger said, 'None of you will have faith till he loves me more than his father and his children.' (Sahih Bukhari)

Supplication/Affirmation

O Restorer (Ya Jabbar), how perfect He is, the Possessor of total power, sovereignty, magnificence and grandeur.

25

She who dares, wins

*'Neither their flesh reaches Allah nor their blood; it is
your piety that reaches Him.' (36 Yaseen:11)*

Who would you be if you placed no mental limitations
on yourself? If you could choose who you want to be
and move in that direction? The biggest regret is to
meet the person you would have been had you not been too
fearful. This is my story.

Technically, I didn't embrace Islam as both my parents were
Muslims, and they gave me my Arabic name. In the post-colonial
era, particularly from the 1970s, many Nigerian couples who
were able gave birth to their children in the UK or brought them
to Britain to improve their economic opportunities. I was born
on the cusp of the 70s/80s divide and my fate was no exception.

From the late 60s, thousands of Nigerian and Ghanaian
children were privately fostered by British families across the UK.
I grew up in such an arrangement as my father studied and my
mother worked. Fortunately, my non-Muslim English foster
family treated me just like their own children. When I asked, I
was told they were Church of England adherents, but we lived
secular lives and never went to church. My biological parents
visited us a few times a year but never taught me the Muslim
tradition. For my parent's generation, knowledge of the deen

wasn't as widely accessible as it is today, and my spiritual side lay underdeveloped.

Between the ages of six and eleven, my parents took me to live in Nigeria. I couldn't control what was happening around me, and I longed for my return to the UK. I thought about it every day, and I did return to begin my high school education, and I lived with the same foster parents. Eventually I learnt to appreciate the years I spent in Nigeria.

I have memories of the household waking for suhur[87] and being taken to a large courtyard space for a special occasion once. I also recall my younger brother and I praying one time at a mosque near our home in Lagos. I didn't have any idea what to do or say. I just copied the movements of the imam in front of us. I didn't understand any of the religion. No one explained it. So I didn't really think about it, and when I left Nigeria, I soon forgot about it.

I was fifteen when I first began to understand what Islam represented. I would see Afghan women dressed in burkas walking on the streets, and, although curious, I found the sight a little daunting as a teenager. I thought they represented a stronger version of what I'd seen in Nigeria and didn't think it was something I would ever be affiliated with. It was about this time my older sister returned to the UK from studying in boarding school in Abuja, Northern Nigeria. She was well versed in the scriptures of the Qur'an and on how to conduct herself appropriately within the deen. I couldn't mask the fact I was impressed.

She became my role model, and never once said to me that I shouldn't dress a certain way, that I should cover up or anything that remotely implied her disdain or judgement at my lack of awareness. Little did I realise this methodology was part of the sunnah of the Prophet Muhammad ﷺ. She patiently and mercifully showed me the way by taking me to numerous

---

[87] Light breakfast taken before dawn to prepare for the fast during the month of Ramadan.

lectures, study circles and bookstores. We bought books, video and cassette tapes on different topics, which exposed me to a clear picture of Islam.

As the years passed, the more knowledge I sought, the more interested I became, to the point where I could single out the few Muslims at my Catholic sixth form college. With my new awareness of Islam, I saw an alternative lifestyle to the one I had grown up in. I gradually began to meet more and more people who adhered to the Islamic faith who I am sure had always been around me; I just hadn't noticed them. It was liberating to be able to intentionally think about my life, the wider world and what was to come.

Prior to this time, I thought little of such matters. I was just an easy-going teenager with few cares for the bigger issues of the world. I was unaware that we are all interconnected on so many levels and that interdependence plays a key role in uplifting all of us. The seeds of desire to understand grew inside me, and I was impressed with the knowledge others imparted my way. I remember so clearly the first time I came across the concept of the Day of Judgement. This was the major turning point for me, a moment in which one decision would change the trajectory of my life forever.

I was seventeen years old and in the middle of studying for my A levels. One evening I watched a video I had brought home explaining the various stages of the day of Judgement. It sounded intense and more importantly very serious. It was following this awareness that I took the plunge. I took a deep breath, and I took my shahadah with my sister as witness. I didn't have to, but I wished to officially mark the beginning of a new chapter in my life. This was where my life took an intentional turn – I was no longer sitting in the passenger seat of my life.

I had benefited from a lot of freedom growing up, and I knew this was now what I wanted in my life. I craved guidance and direction; I wanted instruction as to how best navigate this gift of life I had been blessed with. I wasn't remotely religious growing up but remembered from my formative years in Nigeria that mostly everyone had a religious persuasion, either Christianity or Islam. It wasn't till my lessons in Religious Education at school, that I learnt of agnostics and atheists, by which time I was surprised.

Ironically, as time went on, I became a religious sceptic. But the story of Ayub (as) changed my mindset, and I realised that things happen. Bad things happen to good people, and it does not mean God loves them any less. It was not until I went through this thought process that I came to accept this and anticipate that I would have a relationship with God. I desperately needed Him to help me steer my ship in the deep waters of life. I had to grow up and reflect on where I was and how I ended up there.

It has been a remarkable adventure building trust, confidence, awareness and, most importantly, love within myself, for my fellow human beings and ultimately for my Creator.

I attended a regular Thursday evening halaqah (study circle) in Roehampton. A community formed around a love of learning. The community had integrity. It was real, and in true community spirit, I had someone teach me how to drive over the years. I also had support moving house, and I had a birthing partner when my first child was born. I also gained mentors in my personal development. I owe a lot of who I am today to those early days.

Listening to Ustadh Ahmad Pirzada's amazing lessons under the tutelage of Sheikh Babikir Ahmed in his incredible and passionate yet down to earth style was special. His delivery of the sciences of the deen shaped my thinking. Also, silently observing his long train journey home, usually on the last train of the night, taught me to value consistency and commitment. All this helped ground me in knowing my Lord. It showed me integrity. It's not even about what you say but who you are.

The realisation that friendships made back in the late 1990s are still strong today testifies to what occurs when hearts connect. Friendships that otherwise would not have taken place if not for the love of God. A true taste of family, unconditional acceptance, and a just 'happy that you are here' vibe. Regardless of our backgrounds, may all our hearts connect in worshipping Allah, so that feesabilillah comes authentically and organically, without the need to remind anyone. Just like a lover doesn't need to be reminded of the rights of their beloved.

My friend Sultana once told me in the year 2000 as we lounged on a sofa in our apartment in Damascus, Syria (where we spent a year learning the Arabic language), if you could see all the events of your life laid out in front of you (i.e., your timeline) in the hereafter; you would choose *exactly* what Allah knew would be best for you. I wasn't sure I totally agreed with her back then because I thought I had been through a lot, but I never forgot her words.

Twenty plus years on, I can say for a fact her words ring true. I wouldn't have wanted my life any other way, alhamdulillah. It hasn't been a bed of roses, but it hasn't been all thorns either. We take the rough with the smooth, the bitter with the sweet, as everything is known through its opposite in this world of polarity. If we never experienced any pain, we'd never appreciate or know what it was to have ease or joy in our lives. The ayah 'with hardship comes ease' speaks to me that in every difficulty lies a lesson, an opportunity – an opportunity for growth spiritually, emotionally and financially.

A *Prophetic Tradition*

'A Muslim is a brother of another Muslim. So he should not oppress him nor should he hand him over to his shaytan or his self that is inclined to evil. Whoever fulfils the needs of his brother, Allah will fulfil his needs; whoever removes the troubles of his brother, Allah will remove one of his troubles on the Day of Judgement; and whoever covers up the fault of a Muslim, Allah will cover up his fault on the Day of Judgement.' (Sahih Bukhari)

Supplication/Affirmation

Sufficient for me is Allah and He is the best Disposer of affairs.

26

The ancestors

'Worship God alone, do not attribute divinity to others.
Be good to your parents, close relatives, orphans, the needy,
to close and far neighbours, close friends and stranded
travellers.' (4 al-Nisa:36)

None of us stand alone. We stand on the prayers, dreams and wishes of our ancestors. We are the completion of their story, their happiness manifested. We are all part of a long lineage of incredible individuals whose names may have been forgotten, but part of whose spirit lives on within us. This is Mario's story.

My journey started with my parents, who were both born in Mozambique. My father's mother was Muslim and his father was Catholic. In this way, he grew up going to the mosque on Fridays and sometimes going to church on Sundays. As a result, when he became an adult, he didn't impose either religion on his children. So growing up, we weren't raised with any specific spiritual tradition, and my father always said that to have a relationship with God was a personal journey. He therefore gave us the freedom to follow the path we wanted and embrace the spiritual tradition that best suited us. This led to us just believing in one God, and that was it.

Although I was born in Mozambique, we moved to Portugal when I was young. At the age of eight years old, I started attending a Pentecostal church in Portugal with my sister, who was fifteen and had become a Christian. My family then moved to London a couple of years later, and, by the age of thirteen, I had decided I wanted to become a born-again Christian.

I was extremely active in my church. I attended regularly and participated in various youth programmes, and I went to weekly Bible study classes. At the time, I really enjoyed it, but then I read a lot, and things just didn't make sense to me. I asked my church minister and pastor, but I was not content with the answers I was given. By the age of seventeen, I had started moving away from the church and began to look into other spiritual traditions. I studied Buddhism for a while. Then I came across Rastafarianism, and I grew dreadlocks and changed my diet, adopting some of the Rastafarian traditions.

About six years later when I was twenty-three, I travelled to the Gambia. It was only meant to be a holiday for a few weeks, but it changed my entire outlook on life. I was really touched by the way the people there lived their lives. Despite the sticky heat, I saw and I appreciated the way the society was set up. The young looked after the elderly, and the ones that had slightly more money looked after the poor in a very natural way. It was almost as though the heat of the sun warmed the people's hearts. Most people I met demonstrated a notion of self-effacement; I saw such humility. I made the connection that the Gambia's population was majority Muslim. I had heard of a lot of practices that sounded great in theory, but I had not seen any of them in practice until I visited the Gambia.

When I returned home and reflected on my trip, I realised my love for Islam had returned; it was, after all, part of my heritage. Then I started reading more about Islam. I cut off my dreadlocks, and around the age of twenty-four, I converted. I took my shahadah at a circle in London, and the sheikh there gave me my name.

I believe I have benefited directly from my ancestors. My grandmother was an Indian Muslim who was made an outcast by her family because she had fallen in love with an African man who was Catholic. Her family were very clear with her and made their point: 'No, you are Indian. You are supposed to marry within your own people, and you are Muslim.' Despite the threats, my grandmother did not give up on her husband. None of their children became Muslim nor any of her grandchildren either until I did.

I share the same name as my father, her youngest son, and my grandmother and I were very close. She would always place her hand on my head and say to me 'You'll be the one to bring Islam back.' At the time, I was very young and didn't understand. I just ran around the house. It was only after I converted to Islam that I remembered her words, and it brought me to tears.

I do not know if it was my grandmother's prayers that brought me back to Islam, but through me, my father also converted to Islam some years later and so did my niece. It has been beautiful to see some family members return to the deen.

When I took my shahadah, my immediate family was quite supportive, though at first my sisters were a little bit quiet about it. My father asked if it was because of a woman. I told him that there was no woman involved. I felt no pressure in anything, and upon seeing my character change, my sisters developed respect for Islam. At the beginning, they were only worried because of things they had heard or read in the media about Islam and Muslims, and I understood that.

Prophetic Tradition

'He who believes in Allah and the Last Day, let him maintain good relations with his kin.' (Sahih Bukhari)

Supplication/Affirmation

I nurture all positive relationships in my life because they help me reach my goals.

Where we are heading

IN societies where people are prone to loneliness despite the presence of thousands of people around them, it's not a lack of people that is the issue, but a lack of hearts connecting through love and trust. The Prophet Muhammad (pbuh) encouraged us to 'love for your brother or sister what you love for yourself.' In true balance, the Prophet Muhammad (pbuh) also warned in numerous ahadith about the importance of the company we keep because we eventually resemble those we spend the most time with. We know that if we hang around five hardworking people, we become the sixth, and if we hang around five backbiters, we become the sixth. Your network becomes your net worth.

Synergy is real; the whole is greater than the sum of its parts. We can achieve so much more when we work together in interdependence. Combined efforts in the physical realm are a reflection of hearts connecting on a spiritual level. Sayyid Ali (ra) said, 'That which comes from the heart reaches the heart, and that which doesn't come from the heart doesn't go past the ears.' In the soul realm, we were close to certain people, and that's why we feel an affinity with certain individuals on earth for no clear reason, and there are some people we just do not gel with for no apparent reason. May Allah facilitate our paths and connect our hearts in order to please Him. Ameen.

Reflections

About the author

Sekina Yakub is an educational consultant and researcher in psychology and holds a BA (hons) in Arabic and English linguistics. She lives in London with her four children.

'There is no compulsion in religion. Indeed, the right path stands out clearly from error. Whoever rejects evil and believes in Allah has grasped the most trustworthy handhold that never breaks. Allah hears and knows all things.'
Surah al-Baqarah, verse 256

We know from the stories of the sahaba that the majority of them found the message of the Prophet ﷺ when they were young and in the prime of their lives. The innocence in children can easily see the truth, subhanallah. What links the stories in this anthology is that the contributors were mostly between the ages of sixteen and nineteen when they first felt a personal connection to Allah ﷻ. Though most of them grew up in religious homes, the first moment when they felt their heart turn to Allah ﷻ was in their late adolescence, when the temptations to engage in vices are rife and peer pressure is intense.